The Garden of Eden

Paradise Lost – Living a Lie

by

Ann J Graham

First published in Great Britain in 2022

Copyright © under exclusive licence to Ann J Graham.

The rights of Ann J Graham have been asserted in accordance with the Copyright, Designs and Patents Act 1998.

No part of this book may be reprinted or reproduced or utilised in any form or by any electronic, mechanical, or other means, now known or hereafter invented, including photocopying and recording, or in any information storage or retrieval system, without permission in writing from Ann J Graham.

ISBN: 978-1-913822-21-7

This is a story inspired by true events. All the major events happened. Some of the people have been invented while others are seeded from real people and then fictionalised. Some composite characters have been included.

Dedication

To my nieces.

Your mum and I didn't have a happy childhood, but then none of us have had it easy.

'Happy families are all alike; every unhappy family is unhappy in its own way.'

Leo Tolstoy, *Anna Karenina* (1878)

Prologue

On the cobbled city street, the coalman's horn announced his arrival.

'Two bags,' my dark-haired mammy hollered from the window.

By the time he made it up two flights of stairs with the first bag, she'd already put a few shillings on the display cabinet dust sheet near the coal bunker. From the partially open living room door, I peeked at the red-rimmed eyes bulging from the coalman's dirty face. To keep soot out, my mammy, Chris, closed the hall door as I covered my ears to block the rumble of the coal filling the bunker. I was glad when the man ran downstairs to pick up the second bag. Then a shout told us his job was finished.

'See ye in two weeks, hen.'

He closed the bunker lid, picked up the money and pulled the front door closed behind him.

Once the soot had settled, I hugged my limp-looking teddy while my mammy took off the dust sheets, wiped the linoleum and put the dark blue rug back in its place.

The paraphernalia needed for the fire was forbidden territory for me.

Kindling and the axe, usually stored in the bunker, were moved to make room for the coal. If not, the coal covered everything, and that caused a problem.

But sometimes the coalman surprised my mammy if he was a day early. Retrieving the axe often slipped her mind as she scrambled for the correct money. With a full bunker, finding the axe took days, even weeks. Without it, my da, Adam, couldn't chop wood and that forced him to buy a bundle of kindling from the overpriced corner shop.

Hours after the coalman's visit, a key turned in the front door. I opened my arms before I ran into the hall.

'Da. It's Da.'

I hugged his legs to welcome him. He lifted me, then swung me around. I jumped up and down on the spot, babbling and chattering as he tried to steady me. My mammy interrupted my giggles, saying I should pick my toys up from the floor before supper.

Even at four years old, I sensed unease between my parents. I stared at my mince and tatties until hunger forced me to pick up my special fork. We ate in near silence because my da had forgotten to bring bread and my mammy had forgotten to take the axe out of the bunker.

At bedtime, I came out of the bathroom in my full-length pink goonie to see my da opening and closing the coal bunker. After checking the display cabinet drawers, patting tablecloths and pillowcases, he went back to the bunker.

'What are you looking for, Da?'

'The axe.'

'Why are you looking for the axe, Da?'

'Because Mammy is going to kill me with it.'

Chapter 1

My da, Adam Eden, and my mammy, Christina Thom, were born in Glasgow, Scotland, around 1920 into families with strong church affiliations. My da's Irish father and Scottish mother were of a fundamentalist persuasion, while my mammy's Scottish parents were divided. Her mother was a devoted Christian, but her father had no time for such nonsense and put his trust in public houses and philandering.

Any social groups Mammy and Da were involved in had religious ideals. Mammy told me that a church event had brought them together; the Thursday evening Bible study, not long before the outbreak of World War II. Although my da was a handsome, dark-haired eighteen-year-old, he wasn't adept at dealing with the opposite sex, but his slightly shy and serious demeanour made him attractive to my mammy. She was a bubbly and fun-loving seventeen-year-old brunette. After he caught her eye, Mammy took every opportunity to make sure their paths crossed. She sensed hidden potential and, when they began courting, she aimed to help him lighten up.

To a certain extent, my da had been a considerate man when they first dated, but sometimes his generosity was spoiled by what my mammy considered his overly careful spending habits. On one occasion, to her delight, he had bought her a box of chocolates, but the second time he handed over a gift, to her dismay, it was only a packet of sweets. He had already opened the cellophane to try one before he met her. To her knowledge, those weren't typical experiences for young women. If they went out for a cuppy, which wasn't very often, he would produce his half of the bill, then push it into the middle of the table. Plus, he often said he'd meet her then had to cancel at the last minute without explanation. She hadn't minded so much then because she had been in love.

Soon after they met, my mammy's father passed away. True to his respectful nature, my da gave her time to support my granny, Bessie, with burial arrangements and clearing out Wull's personal effects. Three weeks after the funeral, my da was delighted to see my mammy at church again and sitting two pews in front of him. He lost his place more than once in his Bible when he glanced in her direction and his voice wavered as he tried to keep in tune with the hymns. No sooner had the minister announced his last Amen than he took half a dozen quick strides to be at her side. Her glistening eyes opened wide; her smile told him she was ready to face the world.

When I was a teenager, Da told me about the outbreak of war. In 1939, he was nineteen. One day, he listened to the news on the wireless and, as a fit young man, knew he wouldn't be able to avoid conscription. They might force him to carry a gun, something totally against his principles. His only alternative was to sign up before he was called up and join a regiment of his choice. An acceptable option was with the Medical Corps working as an ambulance driver. After a basic training programme in Scotland, he was posted overseas and spent his time between the UK and Europe. Da took his work seriously and looked at it as an opportunity to learn to drive, deal with injured soldiers and maybe pick up a foreign language. He and my mammy promised to write to each other and both looked forward to his home visits.

Once combat began, he was in the thick of it when bombs fell and left a tangle of dead bodies for the medical crews who were sweeping up behind. The stench of death hit him most days; he struggled to bandage the injured while fighter planes were overhead, and the threats of shelling and mortar bombing were ever-present. The explosions damaged the men's ears. Da was numb when he walked across fields to pick out who was worth attending to and who was too far gone. He felt ruthless, but he had no choice; there was no room for emotions. Sometimes he had to pull the bodies of dead soldiers over him for protection, as relentless shelling prevented him from running from the area.

One day, towards the end of the war, Da and his navigator, Nick, were driving in an ambulance along a country road in northern France when they spied a group of men in the distance. Their uniforms were not British, and Da and Nick wondered if they could trust the enemy to abide by the Geneva Convention; it could be a trap, so they discussed what they should do with the group. Drawing closer, Da stopped, pulled on the handbrake, and stepped out. Unable to speak one another's language, he gathered the leader of the group was surrendering, and the men obeyed when Nick indicated they should throw their guns in a nearby ditch. The soldiers got a share of the rations then Da had to get the men to the closest army post for transfer. The group greedily drank what water they were given and Da turned the vehicle around. The enemy soldiers walked behind the ambulance for four miles.

Da felt he'd succeeded, thankful he'd followed safety protocols. However, that wasn't the end. His commanding officer asked about the men's helmets.

'They're wearing them!' Da had responded.

'Yes, well that's the problem. You were obliged to rid them of all guns and potential weapons. You left them with heavy, solid helmets. You'll be reported for this!'

That was life in the British Army. Da witnessed so many atrocities he told me he struggled to stay the same young man he had been before the war.

Meanwhile, Mammy had joined the Auxiliary Territorial Service (ATS) and stayed on home soil. Her tales made me laugh. Cooking, store-keeping and clerical work were part of her remit, but she eventually discovered there was fun to be had when they stationed her in barracks close to home in the south of Scotland. The fifty women from all over the country had expected to start homes and families before they lived and worked together to support the war effort. They bonded and kept each other's spirits up while joking, singing, and arranging nights out. It wasn't that Mammy felt she had to avoid dancing and mixing with the local laddies, she just wasn't interested because she was waiting for Da, the love of her life, to return.

Despite the fun, she also found herself in bother with her superiors. Each evening, the lassies could light a coal fire, provided at least one of them stayed on fire duty. No more coal was to be put on after eight o'clock because the fire had to be out before they went to bed. Happily agreeing to do fire duty, Mammy had watched the lassies depart for their Saturday night out at the dance hall without her. Just before eight o'clock, she noted the dying embers and thought the others might appreciate a cosier fire on their return. She piled on the coal, thinking no one would check, and within half an hour, the fire was blazing.

'Who put extra coal on at such a late hour?' her superior asked as she threw open the door.

'Well, I did. The lassies are out dancing tonight and most of them won't be in until after ten o'clock,' Mammy offered as an excuse.

'That's very kind of you. You'll be pleased to know you'll get the benefit of the fire until it's out. The rule is no more coal after eight and you've broken it. Enjoy your night by the fire. I'll be putting this in the report book.'

The others came in full of stories and thanked Mammy for her consideration on a frosty night. Some of them offered to stay up with her until the fire died down, but she declined. At three o'clock in the morning, she crawled through to bed, weary and disillusioned; she had learned her lesson but laughed at her stupidity as soon as her head hit the pillow. She continued to see the funny side of things and looked forward to the adventures she hoped life would throw at her.

After being separated for almost three years and now in their early twenties, the two married in Glasgow at a quiet ceremony in 1942 when Da had leave and before they both had to return to wartime duties. Once the war ended in 1945, they stayed with my granny Bessie, for a few months until they could afford to set up their own home in the city.

I heard from Mammy that, as a young married couple, they were inseparable and happy. They worked together briefly in a newsagent's shop and had the same circle of friends. One Saturday morning, they took the bus into the city centre and picked up some bits and pieces. Mammy hadn't paid attention to Da's mention of a rare football match scheduled for that afternoon. As they left the shop, he pointed at a bus, explaining that was the one he needed to catch it for the football match. Mammy had smiled, telling him to jump on it and enjoy the match; she'd see him at home later in the day. She watched him waving to her from his seat upstairs. Mammy told me that was the first time she felt truly married because they were now settled and doing normal things.

Da had always wanted to be a carpenter but there weren't any immediate openings for him, so he accepted a job in a thriving nearby shop and, learning quickly, embarked on a career as a grocer. Eventually, his boss reached retirement age and gave my twenty-eight-year-old da first refusal of the business. It was a big undertaking, but he felt he could make a go of it if Mammy joined him. This would have been impossible if they had had a baby.

In those days, despite what they learned in wartime, society classed women as only having skills to cook, clean and bring up the weans. Males were the breadwinners because, even if men and women were doing the same jobs, companies afforded the men higher rates of pay. It made economic sense for men to work and women to stay home and tend to coal fires, going shopping every day, since fridges and freezers for the home didn't exist and washing clothes by hand.

As chance would have it, Mammy's older brother, my Uncle Georgie, hadn't found suitable employment since the war ended. He and his wife, my Aunt Rose, didn't have children, so Da put the proposal of a family grocery business forward. The two couples thrashed out the finer details of how they would share responsibilities. Da knew the trade, so stock-taking and book-keeping fell to him while he put Georgie in charge of ordering and deliveries. The women would serve customers and deal with the rationing coupons. Da was unwavering in his rule that the shop would be closed on a Sunday, the Sabbath. His philosophy stemmed from the general ethos of post-war Britain and a family background where religion was practically the law. Da and Georgie shook hands on the deal and agreed to revisit the arrangement after six months.

I heard from Mammy that at their first stock-take two months after starting up, everything had gone well; the books balanced. However, their promising start waned after that. Now and again, Rose took a day off, but Da let it go; she was pregnant. Unfortunately, after the four-month stock-take, neither the stock nor the books tallied up. Da never mentioned it to the others, not even to Mammy, but he bought and discreetly installed small mirrors at the side of cardboard adverts or next to display items that wouldn't be changed for weeks. He was determined to find out what was going on.

One Friday afternoon, Da was wiping and stacking tin trays when he heard the till opening. He adjusted one mirror in time to see Georgie hovering over the open cash drawer. In two quick strides, he was at his brother-in-law's side. At the same time, Mammy and Rose appeared from the back shop.

'What's happening?' he demanded as Georgie tried to fold a pound note in his palm.

'I'm just taking some of my pay.'

'You can't do that! You can't take money out of the till. That's not how it works.'

Da's fists clenched involuntarily at his side. He looked towards the end of the counter and saw a tin of salmon, half a dozen eggs, and two tins of soup.

'And what's this?'

'It's for our supper! You're surely not going to deny us that? Are you telling me you don't take things for your cupboard at home? We don't have time to go shopping!' Georgie's voice rose with indignation.

Da tried to reason with him as Mammy and Rose stood rooted to the spot and listened to him pointing out the rules. For sure, they could take goods from the shop, but the cost had to be deducted from their pay. Georgie scoffed. Caught red-handed, he reacted in the moment and turned to face Da.

'Listen!' Georgie bellowed. 'We work hard, and we hardly take five minutes off for a cuppy. You're such a misery guts!'

Da was not to be beaten and, with a condescending smirk, hissed, 'Well, if you don't like it here, you can leave the shop keys on the counter.'

Mammy and Rose had stepped into the back shop when they heard a scuffle. Turning around, they saw Georgie had grabbed Da in a rage and was grappling with his neck. Mammy's first vision was of Georgie holding Da inches from the wheel of the machine they used for slicing ham; he let go when Rose screamed and covered her eyes. Da bent breathlessly over the counter. Georgie reached into his jacket pocket, pulled out the shop keys and flung them in the till's direction. He shouted at Rose, who peeked through her fingers.

'Get your coat and everything else you have here. We're going and we're not coming back!'

She uncovered her eyes, then reached for her raincoat and bag. Their teacups were in the back shop; they could stay. After Georgie slammed the door behind them, Da made his way around the counter, turned the sign to 'Shop Closed' then pulled the blind down. Visibly shaken, he picked up Georgie's keys, then turned to Mammy.

'Give me five minutes, please. I need to do a couple of things. If you want, you can go home. I'll be there shortly.'

'What happened? What's going on with Georgie? What did you do?' she asked.

'I didn't *do* anything,' he assured her. 'I found him taking money from the till and stealing the stock. He's just assaulted me, probably would have killed me if he'd got me any closer to the ham machine. I'm sure I should involve the police, but I need time to think.'

He lifted the tin of salmon and placed it back on the shelf.

'We'll need to open in the morning, but I'm not sure where we stand now,' he added.

That night, they slept as best they could under the circumstances. Da wondered if Georgie and Rose would reappear the next day for their Saturday shift; they didn't. He knew he was in trouble; he couldn't survive in such a busy grocery store without help. Bringing strangers into the business to replace them was too risky.

Da was disheartened and Mammy was annoyed, but she couldn't defend her brother. Thinking this would all blow over in a matter of weeks, she spoke to my granny and told her the story. Georgie had also been in touch with her, and the news was not good. He wouldn't be returning and Da was not welcome in their home.

My parents struggled on with the shop for a few months but, after a year in business, the grocery shop went up for sale. Despite the disappointment, Da wasn't ready to give up. He saw an opening to buy a small, manageable dairy and exchanged his hard-earned cash for a shop at the end of a city side street. He proudly painted 'Eden's Dairy' above the newly varnished shop door. From Monday to Saturday, they sold milk, butter and eggs. After a few months, they expanded their business by stocking bread and rolls, and in the back shop, Mammy made jam, scones and fruit loaves to sell.

When Da took a hand-written advertising sign out of the shop window at the end of the week, he saw that, by mistake, he had written Plum Jum instead of Plum Jam. No customer had commented on the mistake and the Plum Jum had sold out by two o'clock on Saturday. Along with Mammy, they howled with laughter. Their successful business and comfortable relationship made life worth living.

Eventually, Da struck on the idea of adding tomatoes and fruit to his wares. To do this, once a week he had to leave home earlier than normal to get to the fruit market, where he would buy two or three small crates of whatever he could carry on the bus. The profit he made on this type of produce wasn't much, but he wasn't greedy. He considered himself to be an honest businessman.

For the next few years, Mammy supported Da in the dairy, but she became restless. When I was much older, she admitted to me that after eight years of marriage, their relationship showed increasing signs of disharmony. The most important issue was that Mammy hadn't fallen pregnant. They spoke to a medical professional who assured them there was nothing physically wrong; they should be able to conceive. His advice was to take themselves off on a holiday, unwind and let nature take its course. They took a trip to the Scottish Highlands, relaxed in the mountain air, and made plans for the future. It worked, and she screamed with joy to find out she was finally in the family way.

Once Mammy had found out she was pregnant, she visited Georgie and Rose without telling Da to find out if there was any way they could resolve things to keep the family together. But Georgie clarified he was finished with Da, the grocery trade, and Scotland. Mammy had looked forward to being involved with her nephew, Billy, but after Rose had a second baby, Margaret, Georgie bought tickets to Australia and a new life. Sadly, Mammy never got the chance to say goodbye to her brother and his family.

I was born in 1951. They called me Alice Eden.

Mammy related stories of when I was a baby and how she enjoyed her pleasantly decorated one-bedroomed flat in a leafy part of Glasgow. Nothing deterred her from bumping my Silver Cross pram down two flights of stairs. As time passed, I progressed to a dark blue pushchair and was allowed out of it to run around in the park. Mammy was happy in her role and life for me was exciting. I could use pots and wooden spoons to make pretend food for my teddy and dolls. Once I was fed up with that, I rearranged the button box while Mammy sewed and knitted to dress me in quality outfits. I remember my pink hairbrush. I didn't mind having my fair hair brushed to within an inch of its life; it always sprang back into a mass of blonde curls.

Da's role wasn't that much different from the other fathers of that era who were often treated as separate units from the family. Strong relationships built up between mothers and the weans, but Mammy could see that Da showed intense love towards his *wee lassie*. Out walking, my mammy told me she watched him beaming with pride as I held onto my hero Da's hand; he could fix everything as far as I was concerned.

They regarded me as a gift from God, so they brought me up to follow their strict biblical beliefs. In the 1950s, it wasn't unusual for families to have some connection with religion because Sunday schools and mid-week children's clubs in local church halls were safe places to send little ones for an hour or so. Older sisters dragged younger brothers along to shout out answers to quiz questions.

'Who built the ark for the animals?'

'Who parted the Red Sea?'

'Who can recite John 3:16?'

The prizes of chewy sweets or bookmarks with verses of scripture encouraged a sea of hands and a lot of jumping up and down.

'Me, me, pick me!' was the usual chorus.

We attended a regular protestant Church of Scotland, but that didn't last long. Da told Mammy he disagreed with the beliefs of the minister and elders so, as wives followed the wishes of husbands, we left and thereafter attended breakaway independent places of worship called missions, worship halls or something of that ilk. If there was a gathering for fundamentalist evangelicals, we Edens were there and my parents sought friends of similar persuasion. Missions and religion weren't things we dipped in and out of; Da's faith permeated every aspect of what we did and didn't do.

Like the other ladies who went to the mission, Mammy wore pleated skirts that sat below her knee or at mid-calf but never trousers; these were classed as masculine attire.

She wore a two-piece beige costume and a hat on Sundays because it was scripturally correct for females to have their heads covered while worshipping. She made sure Da dressed the same as the men who wore suits, shirts and ties, a kind of business look. It wasn't meant to be an opportunity to show off a fur coat or trilby hat. Their dress sense showed that they belonged to a God-fearing congregation.

This was a serious form of worshipping and, although Mammy was slightly more relaxed than Da, she appreciated that the substance of what they taught in the missions tied in with his strict and unchanging principles. All questions about how people should conduct themselves could be answered by looking in the Bible, God's word. Those who had read it thoroughly could argue their point meaningfully, and she heard him debate the scriptures with ministers and pastors alike. She had watched him read the Bible from cover to cover and listened as he quoted chapter and verse to support his opinions. One point that was never contested by fellow worshippers was that Sunday was the Lord's Day, the Sabbath, a day of rest.

Throughout the week, Monday to Saturday, Mammy got up with Da at seven o'clock in the morning to prepare breakfast before he went to work at the dairy. On a Sunday, she was glad that he insisted she didn't need to get up; he was awake shortly after six o'clock, dressed and out before we realised he was gone. With no buses running at that time of the morning, it took him around thirty minutes to walk to the City Hall where he could have a cuppy and something to eat. When I asked where he was, Mammy told me he was a volunteer with a group of Christian men who met to prepare a free breakfast for the city's homeless; the idea was to convert them to

Christianity. After queueing for up to an hour, the poverty-stricken souls listened to a fifteen-minute sermon before they got their tea and bread roll.

When Da arrived home one Sunday, he told Mammy of a man who had arrived with alcohol on his breath; this was against the rules, and they had turned him away. I listened to the story saying nothing. Although Da felt sorry for him, he appreciated that there was the potential for a fight to break out when alcohol was involved. Despite the odd scuffle, there were at least two hundred people who had to be fed. Mammy was proud of Da and his commitment.

Once he returned home from the free breakfast, we got ready together for the regular family service at the mission nearer home. So, the Lord's Day was a long day for Da, but very special.

After I was born, Mammy continued to make scones or loaves at home, and Da carried what he could on the bus to the shop. But, working by himself, he struggled to keep up and, as the months went by, Mammy found it impossible to continue with the home baking when she had a two-year-old me to care for and a house to run. Da needed someone else to help and came up with a solution: he suggested they bring in a part-time assistant.

Later in life, when Mammy told me the story behind the new assistant, I wondered if that decision had resulted in their first major argument and significant changes in their lives.

Da interviewed a couple of candidates and one lady, Jessie, agreed to work three hours a day, which suited Da perfectly. It relieved Mammy that they had help but she never thought about the financial arrangement. It outraged her when she found out what Jessie was to be paid. In their first shop, Da had paid Georgie a wage for him and Rose and gave Mammy a weekly amount for housekeeping, with extra when required. Previously, she hadn't put up an argument, but now what he could afford to give Jessie in a pay packet, shocked her.

'So, you're going to pay Jessie almost £3 a week for standing in the front shop serving customers?' She had stood with her hands on her hips.

Mammy's reaction had taken Da aback. He couldn't understand why she was so mad and saying that she had worked in his shops for years but had never received a day's pay, as she saw it. She even repeated what Georgie had called him *misery guts*.

'I really have to pay her a good wage because I'm going to give her keys,' he explained. 'It means if I'm late back from the fruit market, she can open the shop in the morning.'

This created their first unholy war, where an evening of shouting and screaming dissolved into an awkward silence. Da drew it to a close by announcing that their financial arrangements would change from then on. He would increase Mammy's housekeeping substantially, but she would also be expected to contribute to bigger expenses, such as holidays or furniture for the flat. Things from the shop would be brought home, but Da would deduct their cost from Mammy's housekeeping.

The first week of the new arrangement, Da almost jumped when she threw the notes back at him and argued that she'd be better off doing a job like Jessie's in another shop. His temper rose, and he told her he would have to change his plan. Trying to keep his anger in check, he said he would never hand her the housekeeping again. He would leave it on the display cabinet, and it would be up to her whether she picked it up. He knew for sure she had to pick it up each Friday, otherwise there wouldn't have been food on the table.

In the weeks that followed, Mammy let him know by her smart remarks about how much she was spending on grub and that she wasn't happy. But he had laid out the rules, and she knew he would never break them. Mammy saw he was pleased with himself; he was asserting his authority. Now she would have to *ask* him to contribute if she needed something other than food. He didn't have to hang around too long for her to broach the subject of joint spending; ready and waiting; he seemed to know what was coming when three weeks later she made her move. I was sitting on a chair waiting for my supper to arrive.

'So, what do you want to do about a wedding present for Beth and Edward?' Mammy glanced at him a few times while continuing to mash the potatoes.

Da didn't take his eyes off his book as he closed it, laid it down on the coffee table, and crossed his legs. He removed his reading glasses, then looked towards the kitchen recess. He draped his hand over the side of his armchair, casually swinging his glasses by one temple, back and forward. He let out a long sigh.

'To be honest, I don't want to do anything. They've only been worshipping with us for a few months and they're talking about moving on to another mission. We're unlikely to see them again after that,' he answered.

Now swinging his glasses in a full circle; it didn't look as though he was going to qualify his answer. His mind was set, and his thinking would have been, *If she wants to give them a gift, she can pay for it out of her housekeeping.*

He wouldn't relent; he had already given her his reason, and he wouldn't have cared whether the gift was to cost a few pennies or a few shillings. He must have heard her breathe in slowly to stay calm, but it was as though another person had control of her words.

'So, it's not about doing the decent thing, it's about money.'

Mammy had stopped mashing the potatoes, and I lifted my knife and fork hoping for food. I watched as she raised her hand to her head in exasperation.

'I've given you my answer,' he mumbled. He put his reading glasses back on and picked up his book. 'You do what you want but leave me out of it.'

Mammy had some time at home to brood over her weekly allowance and wanted to get back at my da; her revenge had to be good. She looked at the less expensive cuts of meat and cheaper cheeses; she could reduce her shopping bill. Being a grocer, Da prided himself in recognising good quality food, so she told me he might say something about our supper but that I was to eat it all, like a big girl. She was right. He made some comment that I didn't understand, but it was pretty obvious she'd changed her choice of meat as soon as he smelled the stew and potatoes she put in front of him. As she suspected, he let her know it wasn't great, but he ate it.

Days later, Mammy and I looked on as Da brought a mouse trap out from under the wardrobe; the cheese bait had lured two mice to their deaths. He pointed out the baby, and I felt sad for the wee things, but he explained they were pests and would eat our food. Given the tasteless food we had eaten a few nights before, I couldn't understand why that would be a problem. Although Da hadn't detected any more mice, other neighbours complained they were certainly still in and around the building. They had also seen a rat running towards the outside bin area. During the discussion Mammy had with Mrs Black from the first-floor landing about eliminating the vermin, she mentioned Da had asked her to buy a couple of extra mouse traps just to be on the safe side. The conversation with the neighbour turned to the pros and cons of putting down tar to trap their feet or using poison to burn their stomachs. I listened in horror and tried to imagine having my stomach burned. Mammy found out where to buy the traps. We jumped on the bus one day when Da had gone to work. Once there, she asked the shopkeeper about other methods of getting rid of mice and rats. He showed her a packet of poisonous grains and warned her of how much damage it could cause if it fell into the wrong hands.

She must have already known that poison was a dangerous product to keep in the house, especially with a three-year-old around. She probed further. 'What do you mean?'

'Well, for a start, do you have any animals? Cats or dogs?' he asked.

'No, no animals.'

'That's just as well because if they thought it was food and ate it, they would become extremely ill,' he informed her with a knowing nod.

She bought two mouse traps and a packet of rat poison in a red box. On the bus, she must have let her thoughts run away with her. Once home, she read out loud what I thought were the words on the box.

'Do not let wee lassies touch this box. Do not put it near your food. Weans should not tell anyone that you have this box in your house.'

Now, looking back, she was planning her next move. She had reckoned if animals would eat it, maybe she could administer it to someone a bit at a time, disguised in food. She handed Da the traps and, with a sly look in my direction, said nothing about the red box, which I had spied her hiding behind paint tins at the back of a cupboard.

A few days of complaints and unnecessary comments about cheaper foodstuff tasting like poison must have played right into her hands. I always went shopping with Mammy and had plenty of questions. Normally, she talked me through the week's suppers: soups, sauces and stews.

One evening, we were having my favourite meal, chicken, so I watched her as she brought the dish out of the oven. My mouth was watering as she called Da and me to the table.

'Give me a couple of minutes. I need to go to the wee boy's room,' Da announced.

While he was in the toilet, Mammy brought my three bears' plate over to the table and, for some reason, I watched her as she walked back into the kitchen recess and served up a heap of food onto Da's plate. She reached into the cupboard and brought out the red box. With what she called her measuring spoon, she sprinkled some on his chicken casserole and mixed it in before laying it on the table. I thought about what was written on the box and never spoke. For all I knew, maybe he would like it. He didn't complain, so the following evening, I watched as she let double the amount trickle onto his beef stew.

Days passed, and on the fourth day of his new diet, Da announced he wouldn't be able to go into the shop; Jessie would have to open up. He told Mammy he had the flu and felt sick. His legs were sore, and he couldn't muster up the energy to dress himself. He spent the day in and out of bed, only drinking boiled water with sugar to hydrate himself and settle his stomach. At supper time, Mammy told him he'd need to eat something to keep his strength up and presented him with a plate of chicken soup. It didn't surprise me when she brought out the red box again. Da was worse the next day. I could hear him telling Mammy in a weak voice he was worried about the shop only being open a few hours a day. Jessie had been on her own for a week, so he asked Mammy to go to the phone box and call the doctor in. I was to stay in with Da as she'd get to the phone quicker on her own. Before she left, I saw her wrap the red box in brown paper and then burn it on the fire.

Despite Mammy telling him he should eat while he waited for the doctor's opinion, he couldn't bring himself to let anything pass his lips, not even the chicken soup that she had prepared. The only morsel of food that appealed to him was a half slice of plain bread with a scraping of butter but, in the end, he couldn't eat it.

When Dr Smith saw Da and heard about his symptoms, he decided to get him to hospital for an X-ray. It showed Da had an ulcer and an operation was imminent. Jessie took charge of the shop and Da was admitted to Ward 10 at the Royal Infirmary. We went to visit him and, while I was happy to see him, I saw Mammy sitting at his bedside with a worried look on her face. Her imagination would have been running wild; she probably expected to see a couple of policemen walk in to handcuff her, her dirty deed uncovered. But that never happened. Nothing relating to the rat poison was detected.

It took weeks for Da to recover. He also had a spell in a convalescence home at Canniesburn before he was back to his old self. He had had the ulcer and a third of his stomach removed and was delighted to tell his story to anyone who would listen. The inconvenience of life for Mammy without a man in the house brought her to her senses and she told me she looked forward to having Da home again. He was a lucky man; he recovered. She was a lucky woman; she narrowly missed becoming a murderer.

But all this had a downside. Da became extra-cautious about what he ate and hollered instructions from his chair into the kitchen recess. He couldn't relax and enjoy the odd cuppy or ice cream in a café and he made sure we didn't get the chance either. If he couldn't go, nobody could.

Chapter 2

'Da, Da!' I shrieked louder than most three-year-olds.

Mammy closed my book about shapes and helped me down from the couch when I heard Da's key turn in the lock. He barely had time to take his overcoat and shoes off before my special television programme, *Andy Pandy*, was being re-enacted. Exhausted from a day's work, he fell into his chair and took me on his knee. Once I had sung the four lines of my new song, I snuggled my head against the crook of his arm. Reaching through my blond curls, I felt the roughness of his work-weary hands. I caught Mammy smiling at us for the first time in days as she laid a booklet on the table. She walked towards us then sat in her usual chair.

Mammy thought she had lost weight recently; when she had looked in the mirror, she had said her gaunt and pale face concerned her. I didn't know what she meant because she looked the same to me. While she usually bustled between her sewing machine and the piles of knitting needles that filled the bottom drawer, things were different. For the last few weeks, she had sat around most days, lacking the energy to do much more than make supper. Da was right to scold her and insist she see the doctor, but she was frightened. She must have expected bad news because previously she had been looking in the mirror at a small lump in her armpit. But now she was happy and smiling. Probably relief that the doctor found nothing sinister bolstered her up, but her announcement stopped Da in his tracks.

'I was sick again this morning before I went to see Dr James.' She now sat facing us. 'He told me I'm having another baby!'

They stared at each other. That wasn't what Da had expected to hear.

'Wait a minute. Let me get this right. A baby? When is all this to take place?' He clenched his teeth and made a sucking noise.

Both Mammy and I recognised this as a sign that he was less than happy. I wanted to hear about the baby but I couldn't figure out the atmosphere, so I looked on.

'I'm almost three months pregnant, so they have given me a date in February. Might even be on our wedding anniversary!' she said, trying to steer the prevailing negative atmosphere in a different direction.

'I don't see how we can stretch to another mouth to feed,' he said as he shook his head.

Mammy sat back and looked at him for a moment.

'Would you rather something happened to the baby?' she whispered as she stood up, picked up the booklet *Starting a Family* from the table and threw it at him.

I was afraid. I hadn't seen my mammy as angry before. I emerged from my comfortable position and my da's warm embrace when I saw her moving around. Da didn't answer, so Mammy walked out of the living room; we heard the click of the bathroom door snib.

My tummy was tight, so I went to the door.

'Mammy, Mammy. I want to come in.'

I heard the toilet flush. Then she opened the door. But she didn't come out. I followed her back in and watched her sitting perched on the side of the bath, looking at the floor and whispering to herself as if I wasn't there.

'He must know I need support and here he is, thinking about pounds, shillings and pennies.'

Years later, I questioned my mammy about that incident. She recalled that, in the past, he had told her she wasn't as penny-wise as he. She remembered him monitoring what was being spent on me, but he didn't seem to listen when she had said there was no way around it. Spending was part of his duty as a father. She had known he wouldn't be pleased to dig deeper into his pockets, but she had been prepared to tighten the purse strings. It would be worth it. She had planned to cut back on other expenses because spending on me and another addition would go on for a lot of years.

The atmosphere I sensed lasted days. Mammy didn't say another word about the baby when I was around, but she may well have goaded him about his comment in private. Once in full swing talking about it a long time later, she said she hadn't wanted to let his negative mood pervade and so prepared for the new arrival as best she could. At the start of the following week when Da was at the dairy, she took a small suitcase from under the bed and sifted through what remained of my baby clothes, separating them into piles of what might work if the baby was a boy. In those days, it was given that boys wore blue and girls wore pink. The Silver Cross pram was still usable and the embroidered quilts and pillowcases were like new, as was my finely crocheted white shawl. The first-size baby vests were stained but she said she could have reused the bootees and mittens. When Da arrived home, it surprised him to see the paraphernalia spread over the couch.

'So, what's all this stuff?' he asked.

Mammy looked at him standing with his hands gripping the back of the dining chair and surveying the scene, waiting for her answer. I sensed more tension, then saw his shoulders relax as he realised he'd seen some of the things before. He perhaps realised she hadn't spent money. These weren't new things.

'Alice and I were looking at what we've got for a baby. She likes this wee bonnet, don't you, pet?' She smiled down at me, then carefully placed the delicate garments back into the suitcase before putting the finishing touches to supper.

A few days later, Mammy called me over to the couch and we made a list of what she would need to buy. I remember her giving me a thin paperback book with pictures of babies and strange things that babies needed. Terry towelling nappies and some fresh vests, maybe even some wool so that she could knit or crochet a cardigan or two. She hoped to speak to Da about shopping.

With Saturday supper over, Mammy cleared the table while Da put three more coals on the fire.

'Da, can you read me a story?' I asked, dragging my teddy closer to him.

'After you're ready for bed. OK?' Mammy pointed towards the one and only bedroom where we slept as a family.

I skipped through and recovered my night goonie from under my pillow.

'Da, can you get me ready for bed?' I looked up at him.

All he wanted was to sit down, but my little hands on his knees made him smile. He helped me change and patted my podgy tummy, then took me through to bed with the same book of poems I wanted to read every night. We started with my favourite, 'Tommy had a Sixpence'.

As my eyes closed, he kissed my cheek and stroked my arm.

'Leave the door open, Da,' I said, my voice sleepy.

I was to learn years later that was the night when Mammy was tipped over the edge. As she sat in her armchair, sewing the strap back onto my wee pinny, he flopped into his chair. She knew Da would be desperate to read his newspaper, so she waited patiently to get his full attention. Following his eyes once he turned to the last page, she saw that he had reached the bottom of the sports section. Then, knowing his habit of shaking the paper as he folded it, she caught him the moment before he could start on his Bible or some other theological book.

Mammy held out the piece of writing paper that she had hidden under her cushion.

'I've made a note of what we need to get before February. Some little gowns and nappies—'

'How can you say you need more when you could have kept twins for years with all the stuff that was here the other day?' Da interrupted.

Mammy got up and walked into the kitchen recess. Surprised that he had been so abrupt, she figured he must have been giving the situation as much thought as she had. Picking up a tea towel, she dried the dishes, making an unnecessary noise that would no doubt disturb me, but she didn't care.

Over the years, I came to understand that when she was in that kind of mood, whether justified or not, it was difficult for Mammy to see past her resentment for what she considered a frustrating life and appreciate what she had: a flat they owned outright, a thriving shop and a clean-living husband who provided for us. Had she been given her way, she would have spent money on good quality baby clothes; after all, she was sure they could afford them. Not only was her happiness at the announcement of our baby short-lived, but also the enjoyment of preparing for its arrival had been taken away.

Without a word, Mammy threw the plate she was holding across the living room at him. It hit the fireplace and broke in half. She told me later she could see his shocked face and wanted to laugh. But she was more than surprised when he retaliated by picking up a small china basket from a shelf next to him and throwing it towards the door of the glass cabinet; both smashed on impact.

The slight squeak of hinges caused Da to look up from his crouched position; apparently, I was standing at the living room door, hugging my teddy with both arms and looking at the floor. It had shocked Mammy to see me standing there, but it pleased her that Da had a piece of the broken plate in his hand. She asked me if I remembered the incident. It was as though she wanted me to think Da had been responsible for the floor being littered with debris.

Mammy said she could tell by the way Da slowly put the bit of plate down that he was feeling a pang of guilt on seeing his wee lassie witnessing such chaos. She knew it would break his heart that his innocent child, the one he would lay down his life for, had seen something that he wouldn't be able to erase from her memory. Stepping over the broken glass, he came towards me, swept me up and took me back through to bed.

'Is Mammy all right?' I whispered in his ear.

'Don't you worry about Mammy; she'll be coming to bed soon.'

As he tiptoed out, Da left the bedroom door open without me asking him. When I was older, Mammy continued the story by filling in details of what had transpired. She was leaning awkwardly over her four-month bump, brushing up the shards; she didn't look up when he walked past her for a glass of water.

'Might be a good idea if I did something to get rid of this baby. That might be a solution for everyone,' she shot at him.

He didn't answer; to her he looked stunned and horrified. Such an action would go against their beliefs and, although he was concerned about the cost of his growing family, he would never have condoned what he termed *murder*.

I sensed a calm of sorts descending, but maybe it was only silence. They hardly spoke for three days. Da attempted to interact more with me. Although I had asked nothing more about the night of the argument, he kept a close eye on me especially when I couldn't get to sleep. He was especially concerned about the dreams that woke me and would check on me every time I called out. I couldn't tell him why I was crying, but I always wanted him to carry me through to the living room.

'Is everything still here?' I whispered as I looked around the floor.

Although they were communicating, underneath, I saw my mammy was still seething and my da appeared to lack emotion. When I was older, she told me she wanted to strike out at him. She wanted her baby but desperately wanted to punish him for his decisions regarding paying the shop assistant, the housekeeping arrangement and his castigations about the costs of another mouth to feed. Mammy had heard other people's positive responses when he spoke about watching the pennies. Their replies made him puff up with pride and she felt they fed his sense of frugality, which he wore like a badge of honour. Over the coming weeks, Mammy thought more about what she had spat out at him, getting rid of the baby.

She spoke in confidence to a couple of worldly-wise but trustworthy people – a friend, Sadie, and a neighbour, Bella – about unwanted pregnancies. She heard of methods that risked causing severe damage or even death to the mother. They also told her of a chemist who sold medication that, although not guaranteed to work, might address her problem. Three days later, she bought quinine.

I don't remember being farmed out for the weekend to my granny, who Mammy said came to collect me the next Friday afternoon, thinking she and Da needed time alone to decorate. My granny agreed; paint fumes were bad for children.

A couple of hours before Da came home from work on the Saturday, Mammy took the dose of quinine. He hadn't been home an hour when the medicine showed signs of working. As she told me the story years later, I could see her face contorting in the imagined pain. A tightness shooting through her lower stomach was chased by the sensation of needing to go to the toilet. As the pain increased, she told him what she had done. My stunned da realised it was too late to backtrack. She took to her bed and endured hours of agony while he looked on awkwardly. At one point, he looked out of the bedroom window and into the mystery of the street below. Darkness crept in as the evening sun slowly gave way to a silver moon. A car going by scared a black cat, and he watched as the noise forced it to run into the beam of a streetlight. He wondered about the contrast, light and dark, happiness and sadness and how quickly pain and suffering could encompass someone.

Eventually, Da left to call the doctor in. Dr James examined the dead foetus, which was by then lying in a basin, and told her all she could do now was rest for a few days. He promised to come back the following afternoon.

'I'm not going to the free breakfast tomorrow,' Da had announced before they tried to settle down for the night.

The next afternoon, the doctor told Mammy there was so much damage to her body it was unlikely she would carry another baby. She stayed in her bed for the rest of the day.

Later that evening, Da had asked, 'How are you feeling now?' as he stood over her, holding a cup of tea. 'Do you think you could manage this?'

She nodded and started to pull herself up. He laid the cup on the table by the bed and fixed the pillows at her back.

'Is that all right?'

She nodded again as he handed her the tea.

'I'm thinking I'll go for Alice first thing in the morning,' he continued. 'I'll get the bus around ten o'clock, so we should be back before twelve. I'll get Jessie to deal with the shop.'

She took a sip of tea, then laid her head back against the pillows.

'This isn't what I wanted, you know.'

Mammy told me that was the first time in a long time that she had spoken without anger in her voice.

Da sat on the edge of the bed.

'I don't know what to say. It's not what I wanted either, but I think we've come to a crossroads in our lives. It's done, it's over. We're only going to torture ourselves if we keep dredging it up again and again. Can we somehow manage to put it behind us?'

Mammy said that she couldn't stop the tears; her body was sore, her conscience was pricking her and her heart was breaking.

Both of them were remorseful; they agreed to pray for forgiveness and put their future in His hands.

I was in my late teens by the time I pondered over what might have triggered some troublesome times between my parents.

'Da, would it be too hard for you to tell me what happened after Mammy lost the baby when I was four? That must have been difficult for both of you. She's told me about it and I know she's never forgotten it.'

'Well, you won't remember it. No one tells their wee lassie about things like that. You were seeing enough, and I tried my best to keep things away from you so that you'd have a chance of a normal childhood. I told you your mammy wasn't feeling well and had to stay in bed.'

While riding on the bus to collect me the following morning, Da made a promise to God; I was going to be his future focus. He was prepared to accept that Mammy had had a massive moment of madness – she had been unreasonable in the past but never to the extent he had witnessed this time. It was impossible to discuss what had happened with anyone; he didn't want to air their sinful secret in public. He had to hope this was a turning point for them because he certainly couldn't continue living as they had been; the stress of his war years had ended but, although he wanted to make things work, he worried that there might be no end to what he was experiencing in his marriage.

Life continued as before; Da had to go to work, and Mammy had to carry on being a mother to me. They disposed of the Silver Cross pram, baby clothes and baby stuff. Mammy gave the bootees, mittens, and blankets to a distant relative and Da said he would deal with the pram by selling it.

But all that didn't appease Mammy for long. Before the month was over, she had justified her actions by crying that Da was complicit in the loss of their baby, eventually implying that *he* had bought the quinine and forced her to take it. To Da, Mammy planned to keep the whole thing alive for the rest of her life. If she ever thought he was forgetting the ordeal, she was going to make sure she reminded him.

Da looked down at the floor when he recalled the weeks and months after the pregnancy ended. He waited patiently for things to change and remained silent as Mammy regularly blew up. He tried to excuse her behaviour, putting it down to the tragedy she had suffered, but her vicious words embarrassed and humiliated him. The minute he walked through the door each evening was the catalyst for an explosion of newfound foul language. It hurt him that Mammy exposed me to her behaviour. He was sure the neighbours must have heard, but nobody said a word about it to them.

Slowly but surely, he found he was not only being attacked by Mammy's words but also the violence and destruction of their property started up again. It was as though a demon possessed her and gave her unbelievable physical strength. She struck out at him: a slap here and a push there. He did his best to defend himself without harming her. But he got tired of it all and questioned whether their being together was a mistake.

On a frosty Sunday evening in January, I ran to him as usual as soon as he opened the door, coming in from the service. I vaguely remembered parts of the story he told me later. Before he had taken his coat off, I tried to put my hand in his pocket and he scolded me.

'No, Alice, you don't do that. You shouldn't put your hand in other people's pockets.'

He felt he had done the right thing, but he wondered if Mammy would disagree with his handling of the situation and fire up an argument. He wanted to bring me up to respect other people's property. He hardly said a word all evening, avoiding her wrath.

On the Monday, Mammy was fearsome, and he didn't escape her scratches to his face. It was on the Tuesday after supper when he saw she was holding his notebook of scriptural verses and sermon outlines he had collected over the years; he was too late to retrieve it from the roaring fire. He didn't retaliate; two wrongs didn't make a right.

At six o'clock on the Wednesday after work, Da came home, sat down, and looked around. Barely six months had passed since the incident with the baby, yet so much emotional and physical turmoil made it seem longer. The well-organised living room and kitchen recess appeared the same as on any other day, but he told me he looked at them through a fresh set of eyes. The framed photograph of us on a family day out no longer filled him with pride, and he had fought back tears. He had passed many a contented hour reading the books that now lay dormant on their shelf. This would be one of the last evenings he would sit waiting for supper. He said he stroked the brown moquette arms of his chair more lovingly than before. The flames from the coal fire leapt and twisted in changing colours, imitating his turbulent life, mocking him.

He had looked at me struggling to put a hat on my teddy. Only a mum or dad could understand my chattering. He heard Mammy speak and shook himself back to the present.

'So, will we go to May and Jim's on Sunday?' she asked.

Her voice seemed distant.

'Yes, yes, that'll be nice.'

Mammy turned back to the cooker, and he turned back to his thoughts.

Late on the Thursday of the same week, when they should have been welcoming their new arrival, Da secretly packed some personal things into the small suitcase that had held the baby clothes and stowed it back under the bed. On Friday morning, he said goodbye to Mammy and came in to kiss my chubby cheek as I slept. He prayed he was doing the right thing as he stroked my curls. Mammy would assume he had left for work as usual when she heard the door close.

Years after this, she told me the next part of the story and I could piece it all together. Half an hour had passed before she saw the note propped up on the display cabinet in the hall. Stopping abruptly, she scanned it once. Her face paled and her hands shook as she reached out to pick it up.

Dear Chris,

I can't stay in our relationship the way it is. I thought we had so much going for us but now I can tell nothing I do will make you happy. I can't sleep and I can't work properly. I believed it was God's will that we should be together but now I doubt that. Please take the next few weeks to think about things. I will make sure you and Alice have enough money for food and I will build a life for myself if that's what you want.
Adam x

After reading it for the second time, she was aware of me tapping on her knee.

She sat down on the couch and hugged me. I was half-awake. Mammy's mind had been in turmoil and she looked distant when she told me the story, just as she must have felt when she found the note. Lost in her thoughts, lost without her husband and at a loss as to what she should do next. Fearing that people would talk when they found out he had left her, Mammy initially thought she wouldn't tell anyone. She would be an outcast and blamed Da because he was a *misery guts* who hadn't been happy about having another baby. Eventually, Mammy calmed down and tried to make sense of what her life had become. That night, and once I was in bed, she reminisced about her early life with Da and what she had expected from their marriage. Going from one scenario to the next, she concluded that maybe the things he had witnessed during the war had made him a more serious man than the one she had met in the Bible study group many years before.

Social pressure mounted over the following weeks as a couple of neighbours commented they hadn't seen Da. My granny knew something was wrong when Mammy arrived at her door.

The chair I sat on almost swallowed me; somehow I knew I had to stay still with teddy and twirl the fur on his little paws. Granny listened, but she couldn't help; she didn't understand the male species and didn't want to know, now she had freedom from Wull the philanderer.

Each day was the same for Mammy and I was constantly asking for my da. It was in the evening and during the night that Mammy had time to think; irrespective of how much he irritated her, she missed him. She couldn't go to church on her own with a toddler and Granny was dismissive, using sayings like *you've made your bed, now you have to lie in it.*

Da was a methodical and responsible man, so she said it hadn't surprised her that early each Sunday morning an envelope with cash appeared on the hall floor, obviously posted through the letterbox. It didn't arrive by normal post because there was neither a postage stamp attached nor a postal delivery on a Sunday. There was no way for her to know if someone had delivered it on Saturday evening, through the night or early on the Sunday morning. On the third Saturday night, Mammy had tried to stay awake and listen for footsteps or the click of the letterbox. She wondered if this was Da's doing or if he'd got someone else to pass by. She fell asleep on the couch at half-past two in the morning; the whole thing remained a mystery.

Sometimes she mentioned we could walk past the dairy so that I could see him and likely for her to talk to him, but she knew he'd be busy with customers and she wouldn't allow him to reject her in public. Twice she got me ready to go to the shop, then changed her mind at the last minute. It was one thing to disagree with him within her own four walls, but she told me she hadn't wanted to lose her temper in public; not at that moment anyway.

Da's haven was his brother's house. They were close. Uncle Sam and his wife, Aunt Jen, didn't want to get involved in his marital problems, but they sympathised and always extended a warm welcome. On the Friday when Da left home, he made a quick call from a phone box to ensure Sam or Jen would be around later. On the half-hour bus ride to their house after work, he didn't dare contemplate what had occurred for fear of breaking down. He had served his country by saving men rather than killing them. Once the war was over, he dreamed of a traditional life. He didn't ask for much; peace in his life and an opportunity to worship God in the old-fashioned way. He had made his girlfriend his bride; secured worthwhile employment and finally started a family. After wondering what could be so wrong about being careful with money, he shook his head in dismay. He arrived in time for the evening meal at Sam and Jen's; they didn't ask questions as they showed him to the spare bedroom, which was to be his home for as long as he needed it.

Although younger than Da by eight years, Sam also steeped himself in religion. Although they physically resembled one another, Sam's nature was more jovial. They had the same positive work ethic, and while Da had gone into the grocery business, Sam had made a successful career in horticulture. He and Jen lived in a tied house, which came free with the job, on the outskirts of the city.

Two days after he had walked away from Mammy and me, Da couldn't hold his tongue any longer. He asked Sam if they could take a walk around a local loch. They left Jen baking scones and made their way to the path, which would take them on a slow, two-hour trek.

'I don't know where to begin, Sam. You know what I tell you has to be confidential. I don't mind Jen knowing, but I can't speak of certain things in front of her.'

'Adam, we've had this conversation before. You know Jen is the only one I speak to and we appreciate very much that you trust us. If we can be of any help, we will do our best,' his brother had replied. 'I think you've got something serious to say so I'm going to let you talk and I won't interrupt you. Tell me what you have to, knowing that it's between us and the Lord God.'

'I think I've made a huge mistake with Chris. I've done my best but I can't seem to make her happy. I'm miserable, I'm worried and, this is a difficult thing to admit, I'm scared of her and I'm scared of what she might do to Alice.'

Da was sure Mammy would destroy anything he liked or anyone he paid attention to, and he was right.

He related his conversation to me and how shocked Sam was that he was limited in what he could do with me. He had often backed off so that he wouldn't show me too much affection for fear that Mammy would use me as a weapon. When Sam lifted his hand, Da stopped talking and they both stopped walking.

'I said I wasn't going to interrupt, but really, Adam, do you think she would harm her own child?' He looked pleadingly at Da.

'Sam, this is bringing me into the most difficult part of my story.' My da was almost in tears.

After he had explained about the quinine, the brothers turned towards each other and hugged. It wasn't a common thing for either of them to do but it seemed a natural reaction to the pain they both felt. Jen had lost three babies before she had carried one full term and they knew it would break her heart to know that someone, my mammy, could deliberately do away with a baby. As a loving, religious couple, Sam and Jen had accepted that their sad experience had been God's will; their faith had given them a way to cope.

By the following day, Jen knew the story. She needed to speak to Da.

'I think Chris is ill.' Her voice was trembling. 'Ill in her mind, I mean. I don't know what you can do about it and I know it's something that people don't want to talk about. But honestly Adam, no woman in her right mind can have such intense hatred towards her husband or unborn child over such an insignificant incident as disagreeing about buying a few baby clothes. Talking about how to keep a growing family is normal. She's overreacted and I have no doubt this will haunt her for the rest of her life.'

Jen continued, making her point as simple as possible as she spelled out a couple of options: either Da could walk away from his wife and his daughter for good, or he could offer her a way to continue with the marriage and try to support her.

Finally succumbing to tears, she continued. 'But remember, Adam, the verse from the Bible, "What God hath joined together, let no man put asunder."'

Da remembered the wedding vows he and Mammy had made before God and the Holy Matrimony that joined them.

Jen said he would likely have to forgive her for certain things that she might do in the future if she didn't get help. He was unsure if he could live with the foul language and the violence, but, as marriage was sacred in the eyes of the

Lord, he had little choice. Jen and Sam agreed to join him in prayer and ask God to show him the way forward. Although they didn't bring the matter up again, Da was thankful that he had shared his story with people who believed in God and would support him, no matter what his eventual choice was.

Four weeks after Da walked out, Mammy got a letter in the post from him. He put forward a proposal and asked her to search her heart to see if they could start over. He felt they had the potential to build a pleasant life together and hoped she would agree to try again.

Mammy hadn't thought for long. Reading his letter again, she suddenly felt calm, and the oppression of negative thoughts disappeared almost instantaneously. She wanted to be a happy woman, a complete woman, a woman who had a husband by her side. She wrote and told him that a deserted woman with a child was definitely not what she wanted to be. I remember being allowed to put a kiss in crayon at the bottom of the page before she put her reply in an envelope. I got to lick the sticky glue part. Convinced he would be overcome with joy when her short note appeared at Jen's house, we set off to the post box.

Adam, we'll be here whenever you want to come back. Love Chris xx

The minute he walked through the door the following weekend, I held up a doll in one hand and its detached leg in the other.

'Da, can you fix my dolly?'

Mammy said she could tell by his beaming face that he was overwhelmed at the simple request; he was needed.

They spoke about their lives and tried to consider each other's points of view. Mammy referred to his penny-pinching, and he made it clear that he didn't like violence or foul language in the home. Both agreed to try harder. In the months that followed Da's return, they prayed for forgiveness for destroying a life given by God and asked that somehow they would be given another baby.

Chapter 3

Despite his best efforts, Da's thriftiness crept back in. Mammy was more inclined to see the value of personal enjoyment from coming across a bargain or having a special treat now and again. When she saw a coat for me reduced from £1.10 to £1 in a draper's window, she told Da they would save ten shillings. He told her he had a better way of saving more; don't spend the money in the first place.

Such comments resurrected the old antagonism in Mammy, reminding her of the reason they didn't have another child: his frugal nature. She told him he was being overly cautious with money. He struggled to change his inherent prudence but wanted to keep his end of the bargain, and rather than openly admit he had failed, he tried to redeem himself by splashing out on a small luxury now and again.

For my fourth birthday in October, Mammy suggested a treat at a local picture house, a relatively new place of entertainment. I could tell by Da's serious voice he wasn't convinced that Peter Pan and picture houses fitted into the lives of fundamentalist Christians, but he gave in. They had made the seats for adults so, when I sat down, all I could see was the back of the seat in front of me. Da suggested I kneel up; that worked, but only for a few minutes.

'Da, can I sit on your knee?'
'Why? What's wrong?'
'My knees are sore.'
'Awe, come on. You're a big girl now. I've paid for you to have a seat all to yourself!'
'Please, Da!'

Da cajoled me into trying to balance on one knee and then the other, but it was too much, so I turned to my mammy.

'Mammy, can I come up?'

She lifted me onto her knee, but Da remained miserable until the end of the film because he had wasted money on a seat for me.

The following spring, Da closed the shop for two weeks; it was a tough decision, but he had been working constantly and needed to spend time with Mammy and me plus catch up with some jobs that needed to be done in the flat. On the first Monday of the holidays, we took the half-hour train trip from the city to a pretty coastal town. I clung to the penny coin Mammy had given me despite Da's protest that, at four, I was still too young and not yet responsible enough to hold on to money. He relented when the coin was to be stored in my tiny leather shoulder bag. As soon as we entered the carriage, I wanted to hold the penny in my hand, ready to buy an ice cream cone once we arrived. Da instructed me to sit back on the dark red, velvety seats and to avoid the dirty floor at all costs. The steam train jostled along and once it hit a bend, I looked through the window at the plumes of grey engine smoke contrasted against the low-lying white clouds. Distracted, I dropped my penny. I looked at my da, the fixer of most things. His eyes closed and sighed; he was not going down on the dirty floor to look for a penny and I wasn't getting another one. He was probably thinking he had been right in the first place about me having money, but his harsh look softened as a big tear brimmed over and dripped onto my wee pink frock.

The following week, we took a trip to the beach, this time by bus. It took almost an hour before we saw the golden sand stretching out to the blue-green sea. Stopping at the first shop, Da bought a daily newspaper and bubbles for me. I clutched the plastic tub with pride while Mammy helped me down a few steps to the sand. Da's instruction had been not to open the tub until we were sitting down and I obeyed. With the rug spread and the picnic eaten, the fun began. Bubbles rose high into the air and I chuckled with delight, trying to catch them before they hit the rocks and disappeared.

'Can you do it for me, Da?' I asked.

He took a turn, and I jumped around, reaching for the bigger bubbles in mid-air. Da's warning tainted the game slightly.

'Don't use all the bubbles at once.'

I put the lid on, or so I thought, and we made our way back to the main road to find a café with a toilet. Part way up the steps from the beach, I tripped. The lid came off, and the bubbles spilled out. There was nothing to be done but watch the slimy, rainbow-coloured liquid drip down the grey, concrete stairs. Da shook his head; that game was over; he said nothing about replacing the tub of bubbles.

This time, I quickly wiped away my tears with the back of my hand, trying to be a big girl in front of my da.

My mammy couldn't look at him as he practically growled at me. It wasn't hard to read her mind when situations like these happened. She probably thought it wouldn't have broken the bank to give me another penny or buy a second tub of bubbles. But we all knew he wouldn't throw cash down the drain, or down the concrete steps. He always said he was right about things concerning money.

I didn't want to do anything that would irritate him because I loved to see him smiling at me. It was painful to witness short tempers, hostile moods and violent outbursts; I had seen the mess in our living room more than once. Although I didn't understand what had happened on these occasions, I knew my parents were doing something wrong.

During the evenings, I watched as Da quietly read his book while Mammy sat sewing or knitting, each at either side of the fireplace. I loved the white wooden stool he had made me; he had even painted a bear on top. My favourite pastime was turning the pages of my book at the same time as Da turned his. Now and again, I stopped to treat my teddy bear like a companion, asking if he was OK and if he would like some milk. To an onlooker, we created the perfect picture of a happy family sitting around a welcoming coal fire.

On the shelves to the left of Da's chair were books, big and small. Any time I asked to see what he was reading, he was happy to show me. I particularly liked the big red soldier book because it had images. To me, the black-and-white pictures of men on beaches and boats were amazing.

'Can I see one of these, Da?' I pointed to the set of oversized books on the top shelf.

'I can bring one down, but you can't touch it because it doesn't belong to me. Mr Wallace has only given me them to look at. There aren't any pictures, only words.' He tilted his head to one side and pursed his lips, then reached up to the encyclopaedias.

He was right; nothing that involved Mr Wallace, the minister, was of any interest to me. But I had learned something: these were special books, and that's why they were on a shelf I couldn't reach.

A week later, on a chilly afternoon, we sat around the fire, but the usual peaceful scene belied what was bubbling under the surface. My mammy's voice, slightly raised, made me look up from my *Little Brown Dog* book.

'So why did you take them if you don't believe what's in them?' My mammy sneered, looking directly at my da.

After a further exchange of words, which I didn't understand the meaning behind, Da jumped out of his chair. From the top shelf, he grabbed one of the precious hard-backed encyclopaedias. I watched as he ripped the pages out in chunks and threw them on the fire. Once they had disintegrated into grey ash, he burned the cover, then started on the next book. My parents didn't speak while this was happening; I instinctively knew not to say a word either. I glanced at Mammy, who continued knitting without looking up. My body tensed as rage accompanied the tearing of each book; the sparks and flames threatened to engulf the room. I was eventually ushered through to bed but lay awake listening to them shouting for what seemed like hours.

All was calm by the next day, but a similar event occurred two weeks later. We set the same scene in front of the fire: Mammy embroidered a tablecloth and Da read a book. Once again, after a short exchange of words about something that was over my head, I tensed when, as quick as a flash, Da got out of his seat, grabbed the tablecloth from Mammy's hands, bundled it up and stuck it on top of the flames. I watched as he held it there long enough to catch fire, then thrust it against her chest and face. She grabbed the cloth, whipped it away from her body, threw it on the side of the fireplace, then patted down her clothes to make sure they weren't burning. A split second later, I saw Mammy lean over and pick the tablecloth up, put it on the fire just as Da had done, and throw it back at him. I froze. It was a miracle that nobody suffered burns. I could tell they were not only arguing but also trying to destroy each other.

During intense disagreements, I noticed Da would become quiet and suck his lips in; after which he could become raging and destructive. I didn't see him burn anything again, but when they argued, he picked up Mammy's favourite things, like matching plates or trinkets, and dropped them on the fireplace tiles so that they broke.

And so, as a child, I learned to read my parents. I sensed the tension before violence broke out but couldn't do or say anything to help. I told no one what happened in our house; there were too many things going on. It was as though there wasn't time to process any one event because the next quickly overtook it.

As was normal in the 1950s, Mammy endured the restrictions that came along with a young family. To her, males were freer in spirit and movement. She watched Da going to work, to the mission, or to visit his side of the family. When he offered to watch me now and again to let her go out to the women'' meeting at the mission, she said she jumped at the chance to have a break. She also had a few friends, Madge, Betty and Sadie, who, although good-living women, only attended the mission sporadically. Da let her know he wasn't overly happy with her choice of companions, but she stuck to her guns; she needed company. The small group met occasionally, and my mammy found their stories amusing.

At thirty-five years old, Mammy hadn't felt she had much going for her apart from being a mother. I learned that, at school, the teachers didn't educate her to achieve her fullest potential because she couldn't see the blackboard and she lost many years of schooling until somebody realised she needed glasses. After that, she wore specs all her life.

Also, as an adult, she became more conscious of her birthmark, a port-wine stain that covered the right-hand side of her face. She explained it hadn't bothered her much until a woman approached her at a bus station, apologising in advance for her boldness. She told Mammy she'd had a port-wine stain removed and, rather than solve the problem, she'd ended up with a facial scar that nothing could disguise. Mammy went home and thought about her looks, her glasses, and her birthmark. For the first time in her life, she bought stage make-up for actors, which did a wonderful job of covering the birthmark; but *she* knew it was there, and I watched one day as she put on the cream-coloured paste.

'I wonder if I've ever been bonnie?' She contemplated her reflection for a moment longer than usual.

On Saturdays, Da went to open the dairy early and, around ten in the morning, Mammy took me down there to play outside with the local children. She baked in the back shop or helped serve the customers. But from Monday to Friday, Da continued the working arrangement with the young shop assistant, Jessie, and Mammy's mind continually reeled. It was one thing to be paying Jessie a wage, but she was convinced Da was also paying her attention. Now and again, I heard her share her dilemma discreetly with friends. She thought I didn't know who she was referring to when she said he was a handsome, polite man and Jessie was an attractive blonde. Mammy visualised him holding a door open for her or chit-chatting when the customers had gone.

Da came home one night to face an extremely hostile wife. The first sign that something wasn't right was when I saw her stirring the vegetable broth in an oversized soup pot without looking up. When Da greeted her with his usual hello, she grunted. He ignored it. After hugging me, he grabbed the newspaper from his coat pocket, then sat down in his armchair. I saw him staring at Mammy. Years later, I asked him about it because the incident stuck in my mind.

'I remember staring at her on that occasion, and to be honest, I did that often. I could tell when she was unhappy and ready to blow up. The signs were always there. Not always the same signs, but something warned me that an argument was brewing, and I watched her closely, wondering what I'd got myself into.'

Mammy wouldn't have known that he was looking at her more intently than before, contemplating. He said his typical thoughts were about the woman who stood before him, his wife of almost fourteen years, who gave him the impression that she despised him. He didn't always know what had caused the hostility. The night I was referring to, he had opened his newspaper but, instead of reading, he peeked over the top of the page to take in her profile.

His description of her intrigued me. Wavy brown hair framed the round face that he still found pretty. Shorter than the average woman, it didn't take many extra pounds for her to appear plump, but that wasn't unattractive to him. Her choice of blouse and mid-calf-length skirt gave her a neat appearance; the wrap-around apron pulled everything together at her waist. If only he could get inside her head to find out what was bothering her.

'Is something wrong?' he finally piped up.

A split-second too long passed before she replied, 'No'

'Well, if you don't tell me what it is, how am I supposed to deal with it?'

'I already said, "No" Is that not enough for you?'

Da was tired and hungry and told me he had had two choices; accept the silent treatment or start further discussion. The problem was, irrespective of his choice, a full-blown argument could develop, resulting in more broken china and shattered glass. As he waited to see what developed over supper; he started on the inside pages of his newspaper. Out of the corner of his eye, he watched as Mammy put a plate of soup at his place on the table, then continued to bustle around in the kitchen recess. He didn't want to be rude and go to the table first, so he spoke from his armchair.

'Is that it ready?'

No answer. I remember Mammy putting the main meals on the table and calling me over. I saw Da closing his eyes in despair. As he recalled the event, he said his thoughts were the same as many times before. He would have to gulp the soup down, otherwise his second course would be cold. He had already told her that eating his food too quickly would affect his stomach. And so another ruined meal materialised but, before they had finished eating, Da found out the reason for her unhappy mood.

Mammy had done a washing earlier in the day. Before domestic washing machines were available, like most other women, she used double ceramic sinks; hers were under the living room window. She washed in one sink, fed the clothes through the wringer and rinsed in the other. It was her day to use the clothes poles in the backcourt and the favourable weather delighted her. I had watched her as she picked up Da's good cardigan. While humming to herself, she double-checked the pockets and discovered a folded piece of paper.

Mary McDuff, 29 Mull Street

'That's not Adam's handwriting! That's on the other side of the city. I wonder what that's all about?' she said to no one in particular.

At first glance, and with no immediate answers, she spoke out loud again.

'Maybe it's someone who wants to help at the mission or deliver tracts.'

But the name and address preyed on her mind all afternoon; she couldn't shift her negative thoughts about what Mary McDuff might be up to and now and again she picked up the paper and muttered a few words which I didn't understand. She had become angrier as the day went on and when Da finally walked through the door, her knuckles went white as she continued stirring the soup with a wooden spoon. It was as though she was resisting the temptation to throw the pot at him.

After supper, as she picked up the empty plates from the table, she broke her silence.

'I found this and wondered if it was yours?'

Tossing the piece of paper in front of him, there was a flash of recognition as he unfolded it.

'Chris, it's nothing untoward. Jessie has been talking about leaving the dairy, so I got this name and address from Hamish McDuff. Mary is his sister, and she's looking for a part-time job. That's all.'

'A part-time job? Coming from Mull Street to Thomson Street? Does she have a helicopter or something?' she snapped.

Mammy practically threw the empty plates into the sink; I looked up from my story book.

'Listen.' His voice was calm. 'I'm not going to discuss this while you're in that kind of mood. We'll talk about it another time.'

With gritted teeth, she was now over the edge. She shouted a few obscenities, yelling that he always blamed *her* and *her* mood; never admitted that *he* had done something which needed to be explained. Mammy picked up the small, round alarm clock that sat on the mantlepiece.

'Another time!' she screamed. 'Another time! When will you have the time? Maybe you'll be too busy with Mary. I wonder what the folk at the mission will make of this.'

'Don't start,' he said, keeping his voice low.

But she *did* start. She forced the clock's silver winding handle until it popped off. Holding the whole thing in both hands, she smashed the glass face against the fireplace tiles until the back parted company from the front. With the inner workings now exposed, she dangled the clock up and down, then threw it in his direction.

'There you go. You've got *time* now!' She finished with a sarcastic smile.

'If I don't wake up tomorrow for work, there'll be consequences.' He shook his head despairingly.

They spent the rest of the evening dragging up the past with insults and accusations flying in Da's direction, to where Mary McDuff was no longer the issue. Mammy continued to goad him with degrading comments about his manhood and humiliated him further by yelling, 'You don't even know how to treat a woman!'

By bedtime, he'd decided enough was enough. Her inappropriate remarks had hurt him to the core. He told her he was finished as he picked up our box of photos and methodically tore himself from each one. Da took their sepia-coloured wedding photograph out of its frame and ripped it in half. He made it clear he wished he could have walked out as he had done before.

But, as he was filling me in on the story, he admitted it had been hard to live without me, his wee lassie and, if their previous separation had lasted, he would have sold the shop and moved elsewhere. That was a mountain he didn't want to climb. He would stay, but things would be different. The shame of separation or divorce was unacceptable as far as their religion was concerned, so the only thing he could do was to remove himself from the photographs and withdraw from any future attempts at placating my mammy. He had remembered Jen's words and agreed she must be mentally ill.

The silence went on for almost a week until Da decided the animosity had lasted long enough. He minimised the damage. One night, he came home and openly laid another piece of paper on the table. There were two names and addresses on it:

Sandra Wilson, 9 Duke Street
Margaret McColl, 140 Duke Street

He waited until Mammy had seen it.

'So, is there anything you want to say?' He challenged her.

'Just tell me what's going on.'

'These two women, Sandra and Margaret, are interested in part-time work at the shop. They live near Thomson Street, so I thought we could talk to them and decide together,' he suggested, extending an olive branch.

They arranged interviews for a Saturday lunchtime while I played outside the dairy. I learned later that twenty-five-year-old Sandra had breezed in. She had piled her raven hair on top of her head. This complemented her make-up-free face. She chatted in a relaxed manner which my parents knew appealed to customers. Her limited knowledge of working behind a counter wasn't a drawback. She said she was adaptable and would soon learn the ropes. Margaret's demeanour was more serious. In her late forties, she had worked in several shops in her time. With a grown-up family, she now had time on her hands and purported to be reliable and trustworthy. Mammy had the last say in the selection. Margaret ticked the boxes and Da offered her the post. Jessie left soon after.

It delighted both to let Mary McDuff fade into the background, but Da had a story about her. He dare not have mentioned it then. He told me a long time later when I was old enough to understand. Hamish McDuff had approached him. His sister, Mary, had lost her job in a book-binding factory. Unable to pay her rent, she was being evicted from her lodgings at Mull Street and planned to stay with Hamish. He was trying to get work for her in his local area. Da agreed to visit Mary one Sunday evening when he would be in the area delivering tracts.

He had kept his promise and knocked on her door. Immediately, he knew he had made a mistake when a slightly inebriated, red-haired woman of about thirty years answered; she had dressed her slim figure for a night of passion rather than an informal interview for a job at the dairy. After speaking to her about work hours, Da explained that there were other candidates and that he would let Hamish know the outcome. He made a hasty retreat. Once around the corner, he leaned against a wall… and prayed. Da decided he wouldn't say anything to anyone. It could look as though his actions had involved him in some immoral activity.

With Mary McDuff and the argument forgotten, peace returned to our home. Despite Da being able to wake up on time most mornings, they bought a new alarm clock. Sadly, the irreplaceable photographs where he was part of our family were gone forever.

Now and again, he would bring shopping home from the dairy and, as always, he took the cost out of Mammy's housekeeping; he never lost a penny if he could help it. With steady profits, we became the proud owners of a Morris Oxford car and a black and white television. The message to the outside world was that we were a God-fearing family with a successful business.

Unable to bear more children and feeling unfulfilled, Mammy looked at other ways of bringing a baby into our home. She spoke to Madge, someone she respected for her wisdom and integrity. Madge was a tall, slim, and active lady who lived with her husband and three young children in a cottage that stood among the nearby tenement buildings. She could be serious yet positive; she could be sad yet tell funny stories that had Mammy in stitches. They were good together. Still in her thirties, Madge was already showing signs of grey hair, but her enthusiasm and energy were that of a much younger woman. Mammy spoke to her in confidence about her situation and their conversation turned to fostering or adopting. These avenues were open to childless couples and had become popular following the growing number of unwanted pregnancies and the difficulties associated with fatherless families during the war. The next evening, she brought the subject of adoption up with Da and he agreed that was a workable solution.

There were hoops to jump through and various background checks were required. As frequent mission-goers, they were off to a good start. Owning their own home and having a business that provided a secure income ticked even more boxes. Because of an unexplained demand, there was a two-year wait to adopt a girl while a boy could be theirs in nine months. Mammy preferred the former and with me, then almost five, already in place. A newborn baby girl would slot in perfectly, according to the rules for adoption. References from upstanding members of the community were obtained and home inspections went on for a few weeks until the authorities finally accepted our name as a perfect adoptive family.

In the meantime, a toddler more or less fell into our hands.

The story behind it was that when Mammy was a child, her mother's sister, Mammy's Aunt May, had given birth to twins, but she couldn't cope. No paperwork recorded the fact that one twin, Jane, unofficially became a sister to my mammy and her brother, Georgie. Jane grew up, married, and quickly started a family of her own.

Jane and her children were extremely important to my granny, even more so than my mammy, her brother and any grandchildren. That wasn't so bad for Georgie and his family, who were now settled in Australia and physically distant. But, although we lived in the same city, my granny rarely visited and told Mammy she couldn't take to my da. I saw little of my granny, who spent her time helping to care for Jane's ever-growing family, my 'cousins'. Jane and her husband Jack eventually brought up a family of fourteen, with only a year between them. As if history were repeating itself, Jane's children became too much for her to handle.

One daughter, Elizabeth, was nine months old when she had fallen ill with malnutrition. Jane and Jack couldn't understand why she was not putting on weight while the next in line was a healthy specimen of a child. Jane finally discovered that each time she gave baby Elizabeth a bottle of milk in her pram, her older sibling reached in, drank the milk, then returned the empty bottle to Elizabeth. This had been going on for months. At that time, there were four little ones all under school age and a pregnant Jane couldn't keep her eye on what was going on. Elizabeth became weak and caught several childhood illnesses that continued to set her back for the next year.

So, when I turned five, I heard that one of my cousins, two-year-old Elizabeth, was coming to stay with us. Mammy still felt pangs of conscience about the loss of her baby, and this act of charity helped to assuage her guilt.

I felt I was growing up; I was to be a big sister. Because as a family we slept in the same room, my mammy resurrected the cot for Elizabeth and found a corner for it. I happily moved to the fold-down bed settee; the experience of having a little sister was fun.

When it was time for us to go to bed, I lay watching Elizabeth clinging to Mammy's hand through the bars of the cot, only letting go when she finally fell asleep to a lullaby. The first time Mammy let go of Elizabeth's hand, she came over to kiss me goodnight. Elizabeth sensed something was different, woke up and began to cry. Mammy had to spend another fifteen minutes holding her hand until she fell asleep again. In the future, she sat on the floor next to the cot until Elizabeth dozed off and, rather than stand up to walk out of the room, she crawled. I knew I couldn't make a sound, so held the blankets to my mouth and stifled my laughs. As the nights went by, Mammy did funny things as she crawled out. Something as simple as stopping to scratch her nose or make a funny face left me cackling and loving the fact that I had a funny mammy.

I interacted with my new little sister as she toddled around playing with a small collection of toys. No one could have faulted Mammy for the way she cared for Elizabeth and Aunt Jane and Uncle Jack visited every month. Although they were happy with the arrangement, they were adamant that her name was never to be shortened and that she would always know who her biological parents were. That was never in dispute.

After several months, the now-healthy Elizabeth talked more coherently and, like a typical tot, copied me. I encouraged her every step of the way; I loved the job of showing her how to eat. She made a lot of mistakes with her spoon, which had me in peals of laughter. Elizabeth would shriek along with me. Life was pleasant because my parents were at peace with one another.

'My teddy,' Elizabeth imitated me.

'Shoes, shoes, shoes,' she said, trying to get her feet into my sandals.

Of course, she heard Mammy and Da and repeated the words.

When Aunt Jane and Uncle Jack next visited, everyone heard Elizabeth saying, 'Mammy, milk.'

As soon as Jane and Jack left, I caught Mammy saying to Da, 'That's it then. She called me "Mammy". They'll be back for her.'

'Oh no!' was all Da could manage.

I saw his eyes wide open but didn't know what it all meant. Suddenly, I wondered if I had done something wrong by helping Elizabeth to repeat unfamiliar words.

Mammy continued, 'I'm telling you. I saw the look on Jane's face. She was mad; they won't wait another month before they come back.'

She was right. Within a matter of days, Elizabeth's biological parents picked up what I considered my new little sister and her belongings.

Mammy said she had felt cheated. Circumstances had again waylaid her maternal role and instincts. There was a gnawing in her heart when she looked at the gap where the high chair should have been at the table and Elizabeth's little pillow lying forlornly in the cot.

Chapter 4

Back in the ATS during the war, Mammy had enjoyed the fun of storytelling with the other lassies who shared the barracks; she had laughed a lot with Jane before they had both married and left home, and now she and Madge shared the same sense of humour. Mammy could talk for hours and, if she was in a good mood, she would tell of silly mistakes she had made and laugh at herself. One day she had tried henna on her hair; it turned out wrong, and she almost fell over laughing when she looked in the mirror. She would dress up in something silly to make me shriek, like when she wore a man's cap and jacket and shuffled into the room with slippers on her knees which made her look like a little man. Sadly, she felt there was no fun in her life anymore where Da was concerned. She didn't connect with him and, when it came to humour, he didn't seem to have any.

In Mammy's mind, he was a spoilsport. In fact, she recalled when they were first married; they had visited her brother, Georgie, and his wife, Rose. They shared an afternoon of tea and scones before Georgie put on his overcoat and excused himself. He was off to the bookies to put his usual Saturday bet on. He didn't think he'd be away for long.

He joked, 'Unless I win! Then I'll be off to America!'

Da didn't approve. Gambling was, without a doubt, a sin. He struggled to keep quiet as his brother-in-law produced a folded newspaper.

Georgie had looked over at Mammy. 'Right Chris, I'll tell you what. I'm picking five horses today. I've picked four I think will win in different races. The ones on this list all run in the five o'clock, so you pick who you think will be the winner. If all my horses come in today, I'll get money back. Here's a promise. If your choice helps, I'll share my winnings with you.'

Mammy had looked at the newspaper. 'But I don't know anything about horses!'

'You don't need to. I'm telling you, it makes no difference to me. Go on; just pick a name you like.'

Da had given a muffled cough. He wasn't comfortable with this at all but still said nothing, hoping Mammy would refuse. She didn't.

'What strange names. OK, let me see. Hovis, Scarlet Lady, Purple Plum, Bad Boy, One Up,' she read, laughing at the selection. 'Let's go for Purple Plum. I made plum jam last Friday.'

'That's as good a reason as any. Purple Plum it is.'

Georgie stuffed the paper in his coat pocket, feeling pleased with himself. On his way out, he had turned around.

'If you're away by the time I come back, I'll let you know later what happens.'

At the end of the following week, a letter arrived for Mammy. My curious da looked on as she opened it. Inside was a brief note from Georgie and four £5 notes. The note announced: 'We won, thanks to you.'

'Can you believe that? Amazing!' Her smile only lasted seconds.

Da was scowling and shaking his head. It took him less than a minute to react.

'You can't keep that money. That's money from gambling. Gambling is sinful and it's of the devil. You mustn't keep it. You'll have to get rid of it.'

This divided Mammy; she knew where he was coming from. Wasn't gambling a sin right up there with fornication and murder? She had scrambled around in her brain to think of an argument in her defence, but nothing concrete would formulate. It was pointless to say it wasn't her who had gambled because he insisted she was handling ill-gotten gains. Mammy knew she wouldn't win. The result was he had stood over her while she tore the notes up into little pieces and flushed them down the toilet.

She daren't decide without him, so she felt controlled. What she could control, she did with a vengeance. Making meals was one of her major roles that had little or no interference from my da. When she became annoyed with him and sensed she wasn't being listened to, she knew she could hit him hard by using food as a weapon. Rat poison was now out of the question; that hadn't been a comfortable experience for either of them.

It was one of those evenings when Mammy became frustrated with his serious nature; the silence in the room was deafening. She served up the food without calling on me or my da or showing in any other way that supper was ready. She sat down by herself. This was now commonplace during quarrels. I noticed Mammy eating and went to the table. Da followed. As I started on the homemade potato soup, he took a mouthful, then let out a surprised sound.

'Oh! Oh!'

'What's wrong, Da?'

'It's the soup, it's cold.' He stared at his plate.

I turned to look at my mammy, but she was eating her soup as if nothing was wrong. Mine was warm, and I assumed hers was as well. Mammy had made Da's supper less enjoyable. He ate the cold soup without another word.

The next day, Mammy was still mad. I saw supper was one of my favourites: chicken with cauliflower, carrots and mashed potatoes. We ate together despite another awkward silence. Halfway through, he let out a yelping sound, one of disgust.

'What is it, Da?' I whispered.

'I don't know. It's something in the food.' He almost choked.

At that, Mammy looked across at his plate as he pointed with his knife to a long white object.

'It's a caterpillar,' she smugly volunteered as she continued eating. 'It must have been in the cauliflower.'

With half my meal left, I shuddered, then cried; I thought I might have eaten a caterpillar. Da put his knife and fork on the plate to show he couldn't eat any more. Mammy continued eating until her plate was clean. She hadn't expected me to react so intensely, but that was a price I had to pay; she had spoiled my da's meal, and that's what mattered most.

It was only a few days after the caterpillar incident that he complained about her forgetting to take the axe out of the bunker before the coalman arrived. She was delighted to remind him he'd also forgotten to bring the bread. When he announced he would visit his family the following evening and wouldn't be back until late, it all kicked off. He hadn't invited her. All she said was maybe he should think twice about going to sleep that night, that she had ways and means of damaging him with weapons that were already in the flat. Mammy sat quietly in the living room while Da searched for the axe. She must have heard me come out of the bathroom and ask him what he was doing. When I had gone into the living room, Mammy was looking through knitting patterns, smiling to herself.

I hadn't known what to do after I heard Mammy was going to kill Da with the axe, just as I hadn't known how to react when they'd tried to set each other on fire. I had seen the living room practically destroyed frequently, and the tension I felt in my stomach at night made it difficult for me to sleep. It scared me to go to bed. To watch it happening was one thing, but somehow it seemed worse to hear them arguing when I was in bed. I felt trapped.

Sitting at the table was the worst time of all if my parents didn't speak to one another. At moments like these, I could only glance pleadingly at them, attempting to distract them surreptitiously from what might develop. By accident, I hit on a way to divert them from their problems while at the same time amusing them.

One supper time, there was no sign of an argument, but I felt something in the air. If both spoke to me while we ate, everything was OK. If only one of them interacted with me, although I couldn't analyse such adult behaviour at that time, it was a sign that there could soon be an eruption. So when Mammy called me to sit at the table, I shook my head in defiance; I didn't want to join them for fear of what might be about to happen. Mammy tried again, telling me the food would get cold. I stuck to my guns, waiting to see if Da would get involved. After the third attempt by Mammy and the same shake of my head as an answer, Da spoke to me.

'Alice, what's wrong?'

I remember smirking; I had got both of them to talk and focus their attention on me, but I wasn't sure how to progress. I had to think quickly because I was hungry.

I replied, 'I'm not Alice.'

As Mammy picked up the salt shaker, Da took up the conversation.

'Oh,' he answered, 'I was sure you were Alice. So who are you then?'

I thought for a second or two. 'I'm Ann, wee Ann.'

'Well hello, Ann. What are you doing here?'

That was too complicated. 'I'm just waiting for someone.'

Da continued by asking me if I'd eaten; I said I hadn't. He spoke to Mammy and suggested that, as Alice wouldn't be coming back for a while, maybe Ann could join them. She agreed. If I liked, I could jump up on *Alice's* chair and have some food. I was delighted: everything was solved. They were both talking to me and I could eat my supper.

Throughout the meal, the make-believe continued and Mammy and Da took turns asking where I lived, where my parents were and if I had any brothers or sisters. My answers were sketchy, but that didn't matter. I had found a way of distracting my parents by becoming Ann.

They also became side-tracked from their fighting if I became ill. There was a time of harmony as they joined forces to make sure I got the best of attention, sparing no expense to ensure I was healthy.

Before vaccinations were standard, the usual childhood illnesses did their rounds: mumps, chickenpox and measles. Once I started school, I caught them all. Some parents heeded old wives' tales of cures, while others let their infected children mix with all and sundry. Without the internet, social media or up-to-date medical reports, parents relied on doctors and their house calls. It was impossible to isolate with the standard four or five children in a one- or two-bedroomed flat. They normally left a fevered child to come through it on their own while mothers and grandmothers mopped the child's brow with cold compresses or applied poultices.

When I was five years old, I started school. Hardly there a month, I contracted measles. Spots, a temperature and a poor appetite confined me to bed. I enjoyed every minute as they rallied round to fuss over me and, despite Da's usual manner of knowing what to do about most things medical, he had to leave me in Mammy's care. She looked after me as best she could. One old wives' tale was to keep the patient with measles in a darkened room as direct sunlight could affect the child's eyes, causing lifelong eyesight problems. Mammy shut the bedroom curtains, so the room was in darkness when the doctor arrived.

'Why is this room so dark? What is all this?' he demanded, seeing the closed curtains.

'I heard that it's best to keep the room dark,' Mammy replied.

'Absolute nonsense,' he declared as he drew back the curtains, allowing the sun to stream through the windows.

Like bankers and solicitors, doctors were superior beings then. Nobody ever questioned them, not even Da. The doctor's word was law, so Mammy left the curtains open.

After a few days, I was well enough to find my feet. One afternoon, I sat at the table and obeyed my mammy when asked to look at Da to tell him something. He nodded; he could see it too. My right eye turned in towards my nose while my left eye stared directly at him. The sunlight had damaged my eye.

Mammy and I attended an initial appointment at an eye clinic on the other side of the city, two bus rides away, where a variety of tests proved I needed an operation to rectify the problem. Mammy couldn't bring herself to agree to surgery. The alternative was weekly visits to an eye clinic initially, and then a series of drops and eye patches. She understood these appointments would last for years and I was to wear glasses, probably for the rest of my life. I got to choose round, pink, national health glasses and heard Da say it annoyed him it had come to this, but he didn't blame Mammy this time. The doctor had been at fault.

Treatment at the clinic started with eye exercises where I had to look through a lens attached to a machine; I manipulated handles to bring two pictures together and particularly enjoyed putting a soldier in a sentry box. But I didn't like the eye drops. Some went in at the hospital visit, then once a week at home until the next appointment.

The downside was I became known as s*pecky* at school, but the upside was that every month I had a half-day off to attend the clinic. At appointments when I had eye drops, I couldn't go back to school because of my blurry eyes. On leaving the hospital, Mammy would buy me a comic, but I couldn't see clearly until the next day, so it wasn't much of a treat.

The drops eventually gave way to an eye patch, which had to be worn under my glasses over one eye. Then, every few days, it was swapped over to the other eye. Eventually, the eye patch was cut smaller and stuck on one lens at a time, allowing a restricted amount of daylight to filter in.

The role of being my nurse stimulated Mammy's motherly instincts. Both she and Da gave me more consideration and tried to boost my confidence. Thanks to my eye problem and my becoming Ann now and again, it reduced the number of days they spent arguing and fighting.

Once I had been at school for a few months, I was aware of a handful of children walking down the street at the same time as Mammy and me in the mornings. Their school uniforms differed from mine.

'Where are these boys and girls going, Mammy?'

'They go to a different school further along the road.'

Later that day, I was to learn from Da that these children were of a different religion and I wouldn't be able to play with them because they worshipped in another church. He tried to explain to me that throughout the city there were Catholic schools and Protestant schools, primaries and secondaries.

Children cottoned on to how important it was to support a particular football team, reinforcing the underlying bigotry and hatred that existed in the city between the two religions. Da knew the unacceptable day would come when I would meet and probably want to make friends with a Catholic child. For this reason, he always asked what my little friends' names were practically the second they had crossed the threshold. If a child had answered Theresa O'Reilly, a catholic name for sure, he discouraged me from playing with her.

My mammy was glad they hadn't stopped the adoption process when Elizabeth appeared. At that time, they still had almost a year to wait for a baby girl, and once Elizabeth left, Mammy's restlessness manifested itself in anger.

Although the neighbours must have been aware of the heated arguments, they didn't get involved; the order of the day was to keep your head down and mind your own business. Family and friends who knew of the adoption application firmly believed this was the way forward for my mammy and my da.

Time marched on and the wait to adopt ended. Mammy asked me if I would like a baby sister. At six years old, my eyes lit up at the thought. I didn't know that a real baby was about to appear until a few days before it happened.

Once the baby was born, a letter announced an appointment at the maternity hospital. Days before our allocated slot, I picked out my fancy frock and cardigan, ready to impress our new baby.

'Mammy, I think our new baby might like this. Can I take it to the hostipal?'

Da didn't correct my mistake. He must have recognised my enthusiasm. Mammy suggested the baby might be too small to hold the oversized doll I had dressed in a coat and hat.

'Let's take something smaller, something we can fit in here.'

Her brown shoulder bag limited my choice, so I stuffed a wooden Pinocchio into the side pocket the day before we set off.

On a chilly December afternoon, we wrapped up in warm coats, hats and gloves, then set off to the bus stop.

I don't remember the journey, but the sight of the revolving doors to the massive grey maternity hospital on Duke Street will stay with me forever. Da told me to push them round and the intrigue of the entrance almost overtook the excitement of why we were there.

Finally, the staff showed us into a private room where a nurse held our new arrival. Ten years later, I was told the baby's mother had given her up for adoption because she hadn't been married to the father. Mammy held the baby first while I sat expectantly for my turn with the bows at the bottom of my fancy frock pulled down over my knees so that they wouldn't hurt our baby. When I held her, I laughed out loud. I thought my new sister was a bit small, but they assured me she would grow into someone I could play with.

The nurse asked Mammy and Da specific questions and began to complete the paperwork. Every so often she engaged me in conversation and, encouraging my role as a big sister, asked me what the new baby's name was.

I glowed as I looked up at her smiling face. 'Ann!'

I felt pleased with myself. If the new baby was called Ann, then I didn't have to be Ann anymore; having a real Ann would make my parents happy. Neither I nor the nurse, who was busy filling in the last details, noticed my parents' glances. I didn't know that they had already chosen a different name for my sister.

Another nurse appeared and took the forms, leaving Mammy to give the baby a final cuddle before handing her back. We were told we could collect *Ann* in three days once they had approved the paperwork. Time enough to sort out the name, so Da thought.

After I negotiated the rotating doors on the way out, I skipped down the hospital steps. Suddenly, I stopped dead.

'Oh no, Mammy! I forgot to give her Pinocchio! We'll need to go back.'

That wasn't happening. We weren't climbing two sets of stairs again. I was told to wait until the baby came to our house. I had missed the opportunity to show my new sister that I loved her.

Over the following days, we wiped down the second-hand Pedigree pram they had bought through an ad in the paper. I felt important as I arranged the baby's soaps and creams in a little basket that was to sit on a shelf in the bathroom. When the big day came, Da had to work. They had given me a day off school, so Mammy and I went by bus across the city to pick up our new baby.

In the hospital, staring down at her tiny crumpled face, my happiness brimmed over. I was sure that because Ann was part of the family, Mammy and Da would stop shouting and throwing things and the funny feeling in my tummy would stay away. As Mammy scanned the paperwork that needed signing, she pointed out the error of the baby's name. The staff were annoyed and tried to talk her into calling the baby Iona Ann or Ann Iona to avoid filling out a new lengthy form. She stuck to her guns, and they took the paperwork to be redone.

I understood some of the conversation and sensed there was a problem as we waited alone on a bench outside the hospital office for the nurse in charge to return.

I tapped my mammy's knee.

'Are we still able to get our new baby, Mammy?' I asked, fighting back tears.

I didn't know then that one evening as they sat by the fire, and long before we had to collect the baby, they had run through a few names such as Carol, Jane and Sally but Iona was their favourite.

While we waited, Mammy put her arm around me and explained that the baby's real name was Iona and had only been Ann while she was in the hospital. My disappointment disappeared as the nurses brought my little sister out of the room and helped Mammy to wrap the crocheted shawl around her body, creating a sling.

On the journey home, bus passengers were astounded to see a newborn baby and ladies with oversized shopping bags and ankle boots stopped in the aisle to pass a few comments. Once in the flat, I drank in every movement between Mammy and the new arrival as the baby was fed, changed and put in a wicker basket. Later that day, I kept watching out the window for Da coming home from work. As he turned the corner, I twirled around twice because I had permission to go down the two flights of stairs on my own and run into his arms. He held my hand as I babbled on about the new baby, but, as I skipped up the stairs, I tripped.

Da caught me and said, 'Oops!'

A strange little expression, but I was thrilled with the care and concern he had for me that day, making sure I was safe on the hard, grey stairs. Maybe the baby was going to make a difference, even if her name wasn't Ann.

The new arrival dominated our family as we muddled in to accommodate her. Mammy rearranged the layout of the baby's basket, fold-down bed settee, and double bed to create a family bedroom. There was a settling-in period where representatives from the adoption agency visited to note the environment the baby was in. They wouldn't have been able to fault us Edens. A hard-working father who owned a dairy and a model housewife and mother no doubt appeared to be the perfect parents for the baby. A sister completed the text book, loving family picture. What the visitors didn't see was the turmoil and animosity that went on once they were gone. As the first few months went by, at six-years-old I realised no matter what the baby was called, she wouldn't heal the rifts between Mammy and Da. On and off, Ann had to resurface.

One Sunday morning, I was pleased to see Da was still around. He hadn't gone to the City Hall to distribute free breakfasts as normal. Mammy had commented on him not being involved with Iona, so he offered to stay home and help, although, to me, he didn't know what Mammy expected of him. Even I knew where the nappies were kept. I eventually learned she had completely taken over when I was born, so he wasn't used to dealing with such a small person. He was awake and sitting up in bed, but had made no move when Iona cried in her little wicker basket. I noticed Mammy's face, her lips pressed together, clattering things in the kitchen recess as she made the bottle. Once she fed Iona, I followed her back to the bedroom, where she dumped the baby on Da's lap with a smirk. But he didn't automatically put his hands out to hold or protect the tiny bundle. Although I was now playing nearby with two dolls, I wasn't aware that a squabble was unfolding.

'Look! Look! Look what he's doing to our baby!' Mammy shouted to me.

I turned in time to see the baby rolling down Da's half-bent knees to land face down at the foot of the bed. I saw Mammy had her hand up to her mouth as if in horror at what was taking place. No one did anything to retrieve Iona, and I thought she might not be able to breathe. Just at that moment, Mammy reached over and lifted her. Da's exasperated sigh and shake of his head told a story. He didn't know what to do with the baby, but Mammy knew what to do to manipulate me into thinking he was harming our new arrival.

Iona was more work than any of us had bargained for. She cried a lot at night so our sleep was interrupted and it took a lot of effort for Mammy to get me out to school as well as tend to a baby. Sometimes keeping the house and looking after us overwhelmed her. Although she had wanted another child, she passed remarks about Da's life not changing much but that hers certainly had. She was determined to vent her anger at being left with all the responsibility. She tried anything she could to hurt or damage Da, even if it meant upsetting me or putting Iona at risk.

One day, Mammy had finished making the beds and folding up the bed settee. I appeared and asked where Iona was.

'Oh no! I've folded the settee and she's in there!' Mammy cried out in what I read as a mock startle, putting her hand to her mouth as she had when Iona had rolled down Da's bent legs. Mammy didn't usually make that gesture and there was a faraway look in her eye when she did. She stared at the closed bed settee.

I panicked and tried desperately to pull at the leather strap to open the settee. The mechanisms weighed a ton and normally once the settee had snapped shut, that was where it had to stay until Da came home. It seemed impossible to open and, only after Mammy gave a few more powerful tugs, it gave way. Baby Iona was lying between two pillows. Tightly wrapped in her shawl, she had her eyes closed. Iona survived, but I wondered if Mammy had been trying to stop our new baby from breathing. The day continued as normal and no one, not even me, told Da about the incident when he came home. Something bad had happened and I couldn't understand it. I just knew I didn't want Mammy and Da to fight over it.

Not realising that her unsettled behaviour was veering off in various directions, Da wasn't prepared for what was to hit him next.

Since 1956, news had been filtering through about a spate of killings that rocked the south of Scotland: murders of young women and whole families. Although Mammy and Da spoke in whispers about it all, I picked up the gist of things. We had up-to-date news on our television, but normally around six o'clock, and before supper, Da preferred to point out the more interesting pieces from his newspaper. He read the city was in a state of alarm as the murders continued but remained unsolved by the time Iona arrived in late 1957 and well into the following year. The police were sure they had a serial killer on their hands and appealed to the public for any information that might help.

When I was in my teens, Da told me that in the spring following Iona's arrival, he was then in his late thirties and still working in the dairy.

One Wednesday, he carefully stepped over the empty milk crates on the floor to reach a bag of self-raising flour; the final item for Mrs Jessop, his last customer of the day. He had been losing weight, so his light brown shop coat sat loosely on his slim frame and flecks of grey were appearing through his dark hair, which he thought gave him a distinguished look. He reached for the pencil wedged between his ear and the leg of his reading glasses to total the bill just as the shop bell alerted him to someone coming in. Two men, dressed in suits and dark raincoats, stood back and waited until Mrs Jessop had left.

'Adam Eden?' the taller one questioned in an official-sounding voice.

'Yes, indeed I am and how can I help you, gentlemen?' Da had replied.

'We're detectives from Glasgow City Police,' the second man announced as they simultaneously produced identity cards from their inside pockets. 'Can we talk somewhere in private?'

Da walked around the counter and looked briefly at their ID and badges.

'I was just about to lock up, so give me a minute.'

He turned the key in the main door, put up the 'Shop Closed' sign and took them into the back shop, where Mammy had left some baking tins and jam jars.

The detectives announced they had come because of a serious matter; a recent accusation they had to follow up on. It baffled Da, but he agreed to cooperate, although the men were initially sparing regarding details of their enquiry. They asked him to remember his whereabouts on certain nights, specifically after eight o'clock in the evenings, and whom he might have been with. Da didn't have to think for long; he told them he went straight home from the shop each weeknight around six o'clock except for a Thursday when he went directly to the prayer meeting and was home by half-past eight. On Saturdays, he was normally home earlier than six. Every Sunday, he followed the same routine; he attended the mission at least twice during the day, then went to bed after preparing what he could for the Monday morning. He was unruffled by their questions.

But their requests for information became more specific, asking when he'd last been to particular public houses in the city centre. My non-drinking, God-fearing Da was horrified that anyone would think he might have even looked at a public house, never mind enter one. It was preposterous. Leaning on a pile of boxes for support, he gathered his composure.

'What makes you think I would go anywhere near those sinful places?' His voice was shaky.

From his responses and his demeanour, the detectives were sure they were on the wrong track, so they explained how their suspicions had come about.

They told him his wife had appeared at the local police station the day before to say she suspected him of being involved in the murders. They had been obliged to follow up on the allegation. She had given them sketchy details of two particular evenings when he had come home later than normal, extremely tired, and hadn't brought a daily newspaper. His brown shoes had been muddy. Da went pale. He was stumped for words. As he sat down on an old, wooden chair, the men asked him how long he'd been separated from his wife.

'Separated? We're not separated. I'm going home in half an hour. My wife's there just now, making supper and looking after my daughter along with our baby. Separated?'

They put forward a few more questions, then asked him if he had somewhere he could go for the night. They thought he might be in danger from Mammy.

He didn't have anywhere to go other than home, but they gave him a stark warning. 'Mister, if I were you, I'd get as far away from her as possible.'

He went home and ate his supper. He never told Mammy about the police visit and nothing was said about him being a potential murderer, but it was one of the many things he told me when I was old enough to understand the dilemmas he had gone through when I was a wee girl.

It was in July 1958 when thirty-one-year-old Peter Manuel was tried, convicted and hanged at Barlinnie Prison in Glasgow for the murders. The city could breathe again. The newspapers were full of Manuel's trial because, to nail the killer quickly, the authorities had almost convicted another man who was wrongly identified by two witnesses. If there had been a miscarriage of justice, they could have hanged an innocent man for a crime he didn't commit. Da knew he had had a narrow escape.

Chapter 5

Mammy hadn't upset Da's life enough. She didn't find him an easy man to live with because his strict and disciplined character took the pleasure out of everything. Things were black and white, right or wrong. Rather than talk him through her point of view and help him see the world from a different perspective, Mammy antagonised the situation by bringing up the past or pointing out his faults using cruel and nasty comments.

When her mood turned sour, he deliberately sat back and let her rant on.

'Just dry up,' he would scoff.

These words irritated her more than the underlying problem and, if she didn't get the reaction she wanted, she retaliated. Tampering with his food, threatening to kill him or making powerful accusations, became commonplace. She watched as he became frustrated. His words made it clear he wanted the animosity to end, but there was something in her she couldn't stop once she got started. Arguments continued and resulted in mental and physical abuse on her part. Mammy could beat Da hands down with hurtful words and deeds; he retaliated by using physical strength.

Both of them wore glasses, but neither had a spare pair at home; there wouldn't have been enough money for such luxury in those days. When Da couldn't take any more of her digs and allegations, he became a tiger. Mammy would talk at him as she was doing some chore or other and, if it rankled him enough, he would utter one or two words from his fireside chair, wait a few seconds, then pounce. He was straight into her face, ripping her glasses off, twisting them until the lens popped out or the legs bent out of shape. Without them, she couldn't see a thing and she had to fumble around, not even sure what clothes she was bringing out from the drawers. In those days, there were no emergency appointments, no drop-in opticians and certainly not enough money to pay for a new pair of glasses until a few weeks had passed. I didn't appreciate it then, but that was an evil way to deal with her. Glasses were her lifeline.

Half-blind, Mammy had to botch her way around the house, not daring to go out because she couldn't safely cross a road. Going shopping without glasses was out of the question and so she often sent me to the more costly corner shop to buy a few necessary items. Mammy had taught me to read from the packets in the cupboard to distinguish between salt and sugar or custard powder and flour. Eventually, when there was enough to pay for new glasses, Mammy had to go by bus into the city centre to find the opticians. She kept me off school to read the bus numbers and depended on the conductor to shout when we reached the right bus stop. For each pair of broken glasses, there were three return trips in all. One to make the appointment, one to have her eyes tested and one to collect the new glasses; only then could Mammy resume a normal life. Iona never knew it, but as a tiny baby wrapped in a shawl until she could jump on and off the bus herself, the journeys to the opticians were regular outings.

One day, when I was eight and Iona was two, we were playing around the sink area at the window. Mammy ducked when Da flew at her. I looked up to see her putting her hands up to stop her glasses being snatched. She jumped into the kitchen recess. Da picked up a clock, threw it at her, then sat back down on his fireside chair and continued reading. Mammy had turned as he threw the clock and the winding handle on the back struck her below the eye and split the skin. After careful examination in the mirror, she saw a small piece of metal embedded in her skin. She couldn't stem the flow of blood and knew she needed help. It never crossed Mammy's mind to leave us with Da while she sought medical attention; that didn't happen in those days. The children were the mother's responsibility. There was no babysitting service unless the family lived nearby, which wasn't the case for us. Mammy abandoned thoughts of supper as the blood trickled down her face. I got my coat, and she got Iona ready while Da sat motionless, reading. We stood in the rain waiting for a bus, then made the journey to the Royal Infirmary.

Drenched, we sat downstairs on the double-decker amidst the surreptitious stares of the other passengers. Nobody asked what had happened, they wouldn't. Nobody offered to help, they couldn't. Nobody wanted to become involved, they shouldn't. Those were the days when it was completely acceptable for a man to fly into a temper and injure his wife; a woman with a black eye or blood on her face wasn't unusual. The onlookers might have thought her husband had attacked her in a drunken stupor; telling them that a man of God was responsible would have come as a surprise.

Once inside the imposing hospital building, Mammy asked about the procedure; she was told to go to the emergency room. Making our way through a tangle of corridors, she turned around to see me fill up with tears as the dark droplets of her blood formed a trail on the squeaky-clean hospital floor.

I held Iona by the hand as she hummed her wee tune of concern and toddled along behind Mammy and a man in a white coat. While he ushered Mammy into an examination room, a nurse spoke to Iona and distracted us with the handful of worn books and toys which lay on an equally worn table.

A doctor tended to the bleeding with a dressing as another nurse joined them. Mammy told them her husband had caused her injury, but they weren't interested. This was only another domestic incident; they were used to it and nothing ever came of her report.

Although she had hoped for a more sympathetic outcome, Mammy said she was happy enough that Da would have seen she'd had professional intervention. Maybe he would be consumed with guilt and wonder if she'd told someone in authority exactly what had happened and who was responsible. She wanted him to worry about how she would answer friends or people at the mission when asked about her injury; she wanted him to worry that someone might come to the door to question him; she wanted him to worry, full stop. That was the best she could do to harm him at that moment.

Mammy was no match for Da's strength, so her revenge boiled down to hurting him in other ways; ways that he couldn't easily fix.

More so than little Iona, all this affected me. The primary role models moulding my behaviour were at home and the mission. Being truthful became muddled with being devious. Stories from Sunday school had moral meanings about honesty and kindness, but that wasn't what I was seeing at home the rest of the week. It was easy for me to slip into dishonesty to find out how much I could get away with.

One afternoon, Mammy sent me to the corner shop to buy a box of salt. She gave me 6d, and the salt cost 5d. I knew there was a penny difference, the exact amount needed for a penny dainty. Tempting. I asked for the salt and a dainty then stood outside the shop, savouring every chomp of toffee. The discarded paper from the dainty dropped on the pavement, something else I knew I shouldn't do. When I presented the salt to Mammy, she asked where the change was.

'She didn't give me any change.' The lie slipped easily from my tongue.

Even though I had committed a few iniquities within ten minutes, I didn't feel any different.

The Bible stories said that Jesus wanted everyone to be loving, honest and caring and especially to ask Him for forgiveness for their sins. If they did, they became born-again Christians, saved people. All other people were sinners who didn't even bother to go to a mission. They argued, shouted, and weren't truthful. I found it hard to figure out whether I belonged to a saved family or a family of sinners. I was learning about an unhappy home life, a cruel home life. My parents' behaviour contradicted what a saved family should be, except that each Sunday we went to church where we sang and prayed to God. Life became complicated as the unstable foundations of my world shook.

Da would have said he had good intentions and a good heart, but Mammy saw him as an unpleasant, devious character with a good image that fooled everyone but her. She felt people gave him too much admiration for the way he portrayed himself and was more than satisfied when she got the chance to uncover his darker side.

After a day's work at the dairy, he had told Mammy all he wanted was to park his Morris Oxford in the garage ten minutes away from the flat, come home and relax before having his supper. He had mentioned that it didn't sit comfortably with him if he arrived to find someone else in the house, not that we had visitors very often. On the odd occasion, maybe once a month, my granny used to drop by when Jane's family were otherwise engaged. Granny enjoyed a blether while she held a hank of wool over both hands and Mammy wound it into a ball. They worked quickly and the swaying of Granny's arms prevented the wool from tangling. Mammy said she'd need to start supper, often Granny invited herself to stay. Mammy told me she could practically feel Da´s frustration when he came in and realised he'd have to leave off reading his newspaper and engage in polite conversation with Granny about things of little interest to him.

Her visits increased, and she started coming over once a week as soon as Jane's older children learned to help with the little ones. She would arrive unexpectedly in the afternoon, then hang around until Da came in; we would eat supper together. On the odd occasion, she took the bus home, but when she dropped heavy hints about getting a lift, Mammy knew although Da would oblige, it would put him out. When he came back one evening after dropping Granny home, he told Mammy he was more than happy to have her mother stay for supper, but he wasn't happy having to walk to the garage, get the car, drive her home then do a return journey. He was ready to fall into bed, his newspaper unread.

In the winter, if Granny arrived and stayed for supper on nights when the rain fell in buckets or snow was piled up, Mammy felt sorry for Da. He was soaked by the time he got the car from the garage. After one particularly stormy night, he asked Mammy to explain to her mother that it would be better not to come if the weather was bad or to take the bus home in the future, especially if she was going to visit every week, otherwise he intended to get rid of the car.

'That's a bit harsh. It's only now and again.' Mammy protested.

'I'm telling you, Chris. I'm tired after work and look at me, I'm drenched. You know I have to make sure I don't become ill, otherwise the shop will suffer.'

'But how can you do without the car? You use it for work.'

'It's a straight twenty-minute walk. Now it takes me ten to go and get the car out of the garage. It makes no difference for work. But it'll make a difference to days out for you. You decide.'

They spoke about what would happen if he didn't have the car when the shop alarm went off in the middle of the night. If that happened, the police came to our door and woke us up. Da had to go to the shop to turn off the alarm, then come home again. The only time he didn't come back was if the police arrived at half-past five or six in the morning. By that time, he was almost ready to get up for work, so he left and had breakfast in the shop. It wasn't easy for him, running a business with all the hidden work it entailed.

But Mammy complied, and we made a bus trip over to my granny's flat a few days later. Both of them were in awkward positions.

'Look, Mammy, it's not fair to Adam if you come through the week and want a lift home. Come over, by all means, but if you can, take the bus home. If it's rotten weather, wait until the next day to visit.'

But her words fell on deaf ears because Granny didn't appreciate the inconvenience she was causing. Mammy was sure Da was going to do as he threatened and get rid of the car. She was right; he had figured it would be just as convenient for him to walk the twenty minutes to the shop or five minutes to the bus stop where he could catch the number seventy-three each morning. It would drop him off at the top of the street where the dairy was. He sold the Morris Oxford a few weeks later and Granny had to make her own way home when she visited. Not surprisingly, her visits decreased, but we were without transport.

He made other visitors feel awkward too. Betty, a young woman Mammy had met at a church outing and whom she particularly liked, popped in now and again. In her late twenties, she had never married and, without the responsibility of children, had carved out a niche for herself in a well-known city solicitor's office. Iona, now three, and more so me, at nine-years-old, loved it when our 'Auntie' Betty stopped by. I stood or sat beside her, mesmerised because she smelled beautiful and wore bright red lipstick. She also paid attention to us and usually brought a little gift or a sweet.

Betty arrived unannounced just before four o'clock one afternoon on the off chance that we would be home. That was normally the time Mammy would think about supper, but they both became so engrossed in conversation over a few cups of tea that neither of them noticed the time passing until they heard Da's key in the lock. They stopped talking, looked at each other and then at the clock as it struck six. Upon opening the door, Da knew something was different. No children running to greet him, no voices and no smell of supper cooking. He hung up his coat and walked into the living room.

'Oh, hello.' He frowned at the scene before him as he stood with both hands leaning on the back of the couch, staring down at Betty.

'Hello, Adam. I just popped in for a quick blether and the time ran away from us,' Betty said and smiled up at him.

'So I see,' he scoffed.

I watched Betty as she twisted her gold rings. Mammy knew Da would be tired, hungry, and irritated at his routine being interrupted. He passed a few unnecessary remarks about a long day at work, noisily sucked air in through his teeth and dumped a brown paper bag of mushrooms on the table. Mammy had sympathised with him about Granny, but now she was annoyed that he was being short with her friend.

'See? I told you there was another side to him!' Mammy said, sitting up proudly as if she'd won a prize.

Her glare dared him to reveal his fraying temper. Betty looked nervously from one to the other before she picked up her handbag.

'I think I'll go before it all starts.' She gave a nervous laugh and said goodbye to us girls.

Supper was about half an hour late and by that time, both Mammy and Da had allowed Betty's visit to become a bone of contention. An argument started over his inflexibility. Betty never came again and Mammy lost someone she could pour out her troubles to.

My mammy had no qualms about using us as pawns in her strategy for revenge. It wasn't unusual for her to cut our hair herself, but Iona's hair had grown long because she wouldn't sit still long enough for Mammy to trim it. Da loved Iona's pigtails and if there was ever any talk of cutting hair, he made sure she knew he adored Iona's and it was never to be cut. Ripe pickings for her when she wanted to get him back for his rudeness towards Betty. Later in the week, she bribed Iona with four jelly babies and a bar of Five Boys chocolate. The exact moment to chop off her pigtails was half an hour before Da was due home from work. Then she watched his reaction to the long hair lying on bits of newspaper. He let out a disappointed sigh and shook his head. He knew what her game was; even when she explained her actions by saying it was a tiresome job to plait Iona's hair every day.

As if that wasn't enough, she played on Iona's health to further annoy him. Just before Iona turned three, she had developed a nasty, chesty cough, one that came back every few months and kept everyone awake at night. The doctor diagnosed her with bronchitis. Mammy thrived in her role as caring, motherly instincts kicked in, and just as she had dealt with my measles and turned-in eye, she enjoyed being in charge of Iona's health. Sadly, she used that power to create havoc.

Iona's prescribed medicine had to be taken half an hour before bedtime, but she would scream and cry when she saw the bottle of foul-tasting, ghastly smelling pink liquid appear. With her teeth clenched and lips shut tight, she fought against the dreaded potion as my parents trapped her on the couch. Da held her nose and, the moment she opened her mouth to breathe, Mammy shovelled the first spoonful in until she swallowed it. Then the entire process had to take place a second time.

To reduce the screaming time, the medicine would normally be hidden and brought out while Iona was distracted. A few days after the incident with the pigtails and thirty minutes before bedtime, Mammy casually strolled over to the table with the medicine in full view. Iona saw it, and of course, started screaming. Da let out an enormous sigh of frustration.

'Chris, come on. Why are you doing that?'

She never answered. He had a pretty good idea why she was being so cruel; it was to torture him, not Iona. She wanted to provoke him and it was tough luck if her daughter was affected.

Despite using us as weapons, Mammy could be great fun when her mood was positive. She loved seeing us healthy and happy. We got to join in with household tasks, especially when it was a day for baking. We helped to beat the eggs, sugar and butter, but the best bit was when she turned the mixture into baking tins and we got to lick what she left in the bowls and on wooden spoons. The sugary taste of the leftovers was a delight. On those days, we laughed at Mammy's sense of humour and had many opportunities to see her peaceful, kind, and fun side.

Now and again, she was daring in how she gave us a treat. There was a growing list of worldly entertainment she and Da would never consider. They wouldn't darken the doors of public houses, dance halls or gambling rooms; these were dens of iniquity. Picture houses, although somewhat frowned upon by God-fearing people, were in a different league and didn't seem to carry the same fear of eternal damnation. Cinemas, as they eventually became known, were a grey area for Da, but he had made it clear they were pursuits that the family should steer away from. He'd paid for a seat years ago for my birthday and I hadn't used it; that, Mammy was sure, was the reason behind his opposition more than his religious principles.

The outside walls of the imposing local picture house displayed posters about upcoming films. We walked past one afternoon, and Mammy glanced at the oversized advert for *The Shaggy Dog*. Going against the grain, she wondered if she should risk treating us to a film without Da finding out. She covered every eventuality to ensure our plan stayed a secret. I was told of the impending adventure but warned that it could only take place if Da was never told. Three-year-old Iona wouldn't have understood the need to keep quiet.

Once the coast was clear and Da had left for work the next Saturday morning, our oldest clothes were laid out along with washed-out socks and underwear that should have been dumped long ago. The plan was to get rid of them after the event because Mammy thought they might hold an unpleasant smell. Smoking was allowed in picture houses and, by the time an hour or so had passed, the lingering smell would have penetrated our clothes. Mammy even donned an old blouse and a skirt that might have come out of the ark, items that would never see the light of day again. And so we set off on our adventure.

A gang of children held their money tightly as they queued up to see *The Shaggy Dog*. There were very few adults accompanying them. Mammy enjoyed her rebellion as she tentatively approached the cashier at the kiosk and bought three tickets for the ten o'clock show. We were like scared animals as we stepped inside the darkened picture house; the booming music of the supporting film and buzz of excitement from the other children shook our bodies to the core. Once our eyes adjusted to their dim surroundings and we had taken our seats, we were soon caught up in the atmosphere of Walt Disney.

To the delight of the young audience, the main character in the film was transformed into an oversized, hairy dog when he least expected it. Amid roars of laughter, the audience was able to pick up a few one-liners, and we happily joined in. Our voices were lost amongst the squeals of the others copying shouts of a repeated one-liner, 'It's possible, it's possible!'

With the film over, the three of us again adjusted our eyes, this time to the brightness of the late morning sun. Once on the pavement, I looked around to check for witnesses to the sin we had committed. I eventually found out that while we played in the bath that afternoon, Mammy had taken our old clothes one item at a time and burned them on the coal fire. With no evidence remaining, it seemed a successful secret mission.

Later that night, when we were firmly tucked up in the bed settee together, Iona and I whispered a few memorable words from the adventure. It wasn't surprising that all Iona could recall was, 'It's possible, it's possible.' After a few sniggers when she whispered, 'Saggy Dog!', we fell asleep.

The next morning, Sunday, while getting ready for the mission, Mammy asked me to get my white sandals, at which point Iona announced, 'It's possible, it's possible!'

The whole room froze over as I waited for Da to question this strange new expression; then our sin would be revealed.

Disappointed at the lack of response, Iona continued to repeat, 'It's possible, it's possible!'

She became louder until she burst into tears because she was being ignored.

If Da found out we had been to a cinema, Mammy would have been happy to see him exasperated and stressed. Since he didn't find out, we had lost nothing and had spent an enjoyable morning out. Mammy won either way.

Her wicked streak eventually extended beyond Da and became directed at me.

'You're just like your father!' she would spit out.

I knew how much Mammy despised Da, so it hurt to be compared to him.

Sometimes she seized the moment to hurt me. For example, every Saturday morning, I went ice-skating with my school friend, Eve. Her dad collected me at nine o'clock on the dot and took us by car to the ice rink on the other side of Glasgow. I enjoyed it so much that I was more than happy to get out of bed early to make sure I was ready for my morning out at Crossmyloof ice rink.

By then, I could tell the time and figured out how long I had to wait until the car came. One Saturday morning, I woke up to find Da had gone to work, so I sneaked into bed beside Mammy. We chatted quietly for five minutes, trying not to wake Iona, who would scream blue murder if she saw me leave the house without her. I said something about the ice-skating, but Mammy put on a sad face.

'Oh, you're too late. You've missed your lift so you can't go today. Look at the clock.'

Right enough, I could see it was after nine o'clock. I was distraught. Mammy knew how much ice-skating meant to me. It was my only hobby outside of the mission. Through sobs, I asked, 'Mammy! Why didn't you tell me? I wanted to go.'

'Well, you were sleeping like a wee baby. I thought you were too tired.'

Confused and upset, I got out of bed and stood wringing my hands. I threw childish insults at her.

'You're horrible. I don't like you anymore. I wish I didn't live in this house. I don't like any of you and I'm going to tell everyone when you argue with Da. It's all your fault!'

Mammy opened her eyes wide. 'Oh, really?'

By that time, I was hysterical and had wakened my sister. Mammy pointed to Iona and scolded me.

'Now look what you've done!'

She tended to Iona, then said matter-of-factly that the clock was wrong. It was October, and the clocks had gone back an hour during the night. With a frosty face, she told me I could still go ice-skating. Through my tears, I could see I had plenty of time to get ready, have breakfast, and throw cold water on my bloated face before the car arrived. The fun of the morning blocked out the clock incident, but I had now told Mammy I didn't like her or anyone in the house. She had appeared to enjoy drawing out the agony.

But Da was still her principal focus for payback. About the same time as I understood clocks and time, I was noticing dates. The run-up to birthdays and Christmases was important. Mammy's birthday was on 12th September and she told me Da's was on 21st October. Thinking I was brilliant with numbers, I worked out that if the number twelve was reversed, I would get twenty-one, thus an easy way to remember my parents' birthdays. I pointed this out to Mammy, who agreed.

With Iona, we collected things and stuck them onto card. Mammy knew what was happening regarding our birthday surprise for Da. She watched as we presented him with cards where bits of wool, buttons and cut out pictures were falling off. There was certainly surprise in his voice, but one that I couldn't understand. Each birthday, he said, 'Thank you,' with a sad look. It was years later that I discovered Da's birthday wasn't on the 21st but on the 20th.

The violence had not stopped between them, and Iona and I experienced negative physical effects when we witnessed it; I would go quiet and my stomach would tighten whereas Iona would initially hum a tune, then shake and cry. The drama turned our lives upside down for hours, if not days. But neither Mammy nor Da could stop themselves. They were locked in battle.

When silence descended after a disagreement, it wasn't unusual for Mammy to retreat into our only bedroom, taking me and Iona with her. There was nowhere to sit except on the side of the folded-down bed settee. We whispered to one another. There were few toys to play with and we were too afraid to move anyway. We didn't have the concentration to do much more than hold on to a special doll or teddy bear. A quick visit to the bathroom was permitted, but the prevailing atmosphere made it practically impossible to perform and little Iona often wet her underwear. We stayed in the bedroom for what seemed like hours until the need for even a morsel of food eventually drove Mammy to tempt fate and go to find something. She would leave the room and tentatively enter the living room/kitchen recess where Da sat, usually reading. I was petrified as I waited to hear an exchange of words or any other type of sound; neither necessarily meant that the war was over, but it indicated how near a resolution my parents were.

Normally, we were ready for bed around seven o'clock but putting us to bed became a problem after an evening's domestic outburst because, while I became even more silent and withdrawn, Iona continued to cry and plead with Mammy not to leave the bedroom. This could last for hours and so everyone was tense and exhausted.

One evening, while we were in the bedroom changing into our night goonies, we heard an almighty crash in the living room followed by a shout from Mammy, then another crash. Terrified, I held Iona's hand and took her into the bathroom. When we emerged, Mammy was standing at the living room door.

'Come and see this!'

She helped us over the upturned chair and the broken glass from a milk bottle. I saw the front of the television was cracked. What I didn't know at that time was minutes before, Mammy had struggled to free herself when Da had pushed her across the room and held her by the throat against the door.

We escaped to the sanctuary of the bedroom, and Mammy followed. Under her instructions, we got ourselves half-dressed as she grabbed a handful of extra clothes. She told us we would have to leave the house but never said where we would be going. She put her finger to her pursed lips as she stealthily unlocked the front door. Then we crept out of the bedroom, through the hall and into the stairwell. Mammy gently closed the main door behind us as Da sat with his book in the living room, unaware of his family's exodus. Once on the landing, we quickly finished dressing by the flickering gaslight, only to discover we were missing a vest and a pair of shoes for Iona. The shoes were crucial. Somebody had to go back inside. There was no other solution. I was told to keep Iona quiet as Mammy turned the key to open the lock. After signalling 'stay here', she disappeared inside.

The minutes spent sitting on the cold, grey stairs were defining my nine-year-old life. I suppressed my own terror and tension while I quietly entertained three-year-old Iona to prevent her from humming or crying. Other concerns flitted through my mind as I carried out my duty. What if my mammy didn't come back out of the house? Could I risk pulling the brass bell knob to get back in? How would I answer questions if any neighbours passed by? What was lurking behind the shadows from the flickering gaslight on the landing?

There was some relief as the door slowly opened and Mammy appeared with a pair of wellington boots for Iona. Someone had passed them on to her a few weeks previously, and that was all she could find. We cautiously descended the stairs, me holding the banister and Iona gripping Mammy's hand while trying to negotiate each step with boots that were two sizes too big. Once we boarded the number four bus, I knew we were heading to Granny's house.

For some families, grandparents were a refuge but, given that my granny had taken more pity on Aunt Jane's many children, Mammy couldn't be assured we would receive a warm welcome. With no way to announce our visit beforehand, we turned up at Granny's door around eight-thirty in the evening. I saw her roll her eyes as she pulled her cardigan tighter around her well-worn pinny.

She already had two of Aunt Jane's children staying for the weekend and, despite having two bedrooms and the bed settee already pulled down in the living room, she let it be known that sleeping space was at a premium. Even I sensed we weren't welcome. When I glanced in the mirror over the fireplace, Granny let me know she was losing patience.

'Vanity, vanity.' I was being scolded for looking at myself so I sat down again.

I watched my mammy unsuccessfully appealing to Granny. Our cousins all but ignored us while sniggering at Iona's boots.

'Don't you kick that chanty under the bed with these things. The pee pee will go everywhere.'

They screamed and pulled the old cover up to reveal a china potty partially hidden by the mechanisms of the bed settee.The adults were too involved in conversation to see Iona's bewildered expression.

After a cuppy, Granny sent Mammy packing with Iona and me trailing behind.

'Get home now and don't tarry,' she called after us.

There was no room; we went home to bed.

Chapter 6

With so much chaos at home, I took solace in school life and the company of my best friend, Arlene. We didn't bother too much with boys because our paths seldom crossed. In the 1960s, city schools had separate entrances and playgrounds for the different sexes. Although boys and girls mixed inside the classroom, the single desks were in neat rows and columns, meaning the pupils were spaced at least two feet away from each other to give the teacher space to walk between the desks; they were never pushed together to form pairs or groups. Starting at the back of the room, pupils were seated according to their ability; I was between the middle and the top of the class. My teacher, Miss Hay, was in her twenties, plump, with short, jet-black hair and a stunning smile. She took time to get to know each pupil and consequently made us feel special.

By the time I was almost ten, I was conscious that I was the only girl in the class with tight curls and round National Health spectacles; I felt odd, although nobody said anything to me. All this was exacerbated because Arlene had a swinging ponytail and didn't need glasses. Two boys in the class had glasses, but these were shop-bought rather than provided by the NHS and, to me, they looked nicer. My hand-knitted cardigan from unravelled and recycled wool seemed poles apart from what the other girls wore, simply because mine had a collar and little buttons that wouldn't fasten properly. The brown leather satchel on my back matched what the boys used. I thought I was different in so many ways that it ate into my confidence until a new girl, Sarah, joined the class when we went into our sixth year at primary school.

Years before, the little girl had fallen into a bath of scalding hot water and badly burned the left side of her body, including the side of her face. Most children reeled when they saw her and very few wanted to hold her withered hand when they played games in the playground or in gym class. One day, when nobody would stand beside Sarah, I took her bad hand and squeezed it lightly; Sarah smiled at me, then we linked hands with the other girls skipping round in a circle singing, 'I Sent a Letter to my Love.' I felt my curls and glasses were nothing compared to our new girl's scars.

But other things made me feel different, especially when other children spoke of films they had seen and books they had read. One Monday morning, Miss Hay went round the class asking what we had watched on TV the night before; every one of them had seen something from the two available channels.

I averted my gaze from Miss Hay and the rest of the class when it was my turn. 'We don't have a TV now.' No one picked me up on my revelation, so I didn't have to explain that my parents had destroyed it in an argument.

In the playground, the girls played tag and circle games like 'The Farmer's in his Den' or swapped scraps. This involved exchanging pictures that came in packs like cards to make sets of two or three of the same angel, fairy, or flower design, but in different sizes. We kept them flat between the pages of hard-backed story books which went everywhere with us.

'I'll swap you for a big angel for two small fairies.' I would try to bargain.

We played peacefully and quietly. If we were brave enough to look through the gate into the boys' playground, we could see footballs flying around; the running, jumping and wrestling held no attraction to most of us petite, genteel girls.

'Let's go near the boys' gate,' I would dare Arlene.

Arlene had a brother and could explain to me that the grappling boys were pretending to be cowboys and Indians, cops and robbers or just goodies and baddies imitating Rawhide or The Lone Ranger. I was sure Da wouldn't have approved of such rowdiness.

After playtime or lunchtime and once back in the classroom, we girls were more aware of the boys when a serious fight or an incident in the playground had been brought to the headmaster's attention. Everyone sat in silence until the culprits were identified. In front of the others, at least one stroke of the belt on the hand punished the offender; the two or three-pronged leather strap was brought out from a female teacher's desk or from under a male teacher's jacket. Inevitably, the guilty child would cry and the rest of the pupils jumped as the belt twanged on its target. This was a lot for the onlookers to deal with: on one hand, there was happiness that they weren't being punished; on the other hand, they felt the humiliation their classmate had to endure. At times like these, my tension was not as powerful as I felt at home when Mammy and

Da were in the midst of a battle. They had desensitised me to what I was witnessing outside my home.

I wanted to be grown up and was attracted to the other children who appeared to lead freer lives. Outside of school, they were allowed to roam the streets and play in areas forbidden to me; I was too young to appreciate the risks involved. Da often warned me of the dangers in the city, specifically that we were never far from busy roads. The only way to get over the main roads was by a zebra crossing and following the rules learned at school: look right, look left, look right again. There were no stops/go illuminated signs, only the flashing of Belisha beacons at a zebra crossing.

Along with Arlene, I made friends with an older boy, Dan, who was more daring than us. He taught us how to ring doorbells and run away. I knew it was naughty, so I didn't tell my parents about this new game. One day, Dan said he knew of somewhere different to play. We agreed to go and happily followed him until we came to a main road. Without bothering to walk to the crossing, we dodged a few cars and a bus to reach the grounds of an old picture house, where we did no more than jump through the long grass on the wasteland that surrounded the building.

It took me a while to get home, and Da was waiting for me. I couldn't be dishonest with him and so I spilled the beans about where we had been.

'Aye well. You've done it now, you wee monkey. That wasn't a good thing at all. I'm angry with you. I don't want you to go over that main road again and to make sure you don't forget; you're getting kept in tomorrow after school!'

Accepting my punishment, the next day I stood forlorn at the window, looking down onto the pavement where my friends were playing with ropes and balls. I was told not to go near Dan again and I never dared to venture further than my own street after that. The incident could easily have ended in tragedy; most children would have had to endure a beating, but Da never hit us except once when he lifted his hands to me.

Mammy was chiding him about how much attention he paid to us girls; she suggested he was touching me inappropriately, hugging me, having me sit on his knee or holding me up high. The truth was Da was simply being as loving as he could be to me, but Mammy saw behaviour that reminded her of her alcoholic father. Da told me a while after this, her childhood had left her scarred.

'You know you could damage her with all that touching?' Mammy had remarked.

'What are you talking about? I'd never damage her. Is this another accusation you'll be making?'

Da was livid. He couldn't think of anything worse to be accused of. Mammy didn't stop; she told him he would make me think it was OK for people to get close to me like that. As I walked past his chair, he jumped up after seething for a minute or two. He put one hand on the small of my back and the other on my stomach. He made fists and threw my body back and forth between his hands several times. I could feel the pressure on my stomach. I was in shock.

'There you go. Is that damage enough for you?' he shouted over at Mammy.

She was speechless. It seemed the only way he knew to shut her up.

But it appeared Mammy could be more sympathetic than Da. One day as I played in the street, it surprised me to see my teacher walking towards me. It seemed strange that Miss Hay would be anywhere other than behind her desk. She asked where one of my classmates, Greg Black, lived, then disappeared around the corner at the top of the street.

I ran upstairs to share the mystery of Greg with my mammy.

'Mammy, Mammy. Guess who's looking for Greg Black?'

But that news didn't surprise Mammy because she could tell me what had happened a few days beforehand.

During a game of cowboys and Indians, ten-year-old Greg and some friends had ventured to a nearby bridge where a railway line ran underneath. Often, children would watch the trains as they hurtled by, throwing up thick, dirty smoke from the coals that fired the engines. After watching a cowboy film in the picture house, Greg had decided he would imitate the hero and jump from the bridge onto a moving train to get away from imaginary Indians. He had sustained such serious injuries that he lost one leg and the other foot.

When Da heard of the incident, he reminded us that films and picture houses were of the devil and this was exactly what could come from worldly pursuits. I could tell Mammy seemed to have more compassion. She wiped a tear away.

'To think that boy will have to live with this for the rest of his life. What a tragedy.'

When there was no tense atmosphere, we ate our main meals together and chatted at the dining table. For dessert, Iona and I would sit on our little home-made stools at the coffee table. We felt special in our own space.

Iona was often prone to going into a daydream, and even waving hands in front of her face didn't always snap her out of it. One day at the coffee table, the segments of an orange engrossed me until, looking up for a moment, I saw Iona had laid her head back onto the couch and was staring up at the ceiling. It was an unusual position and, thinking she was day-dreaming again, I quietly tried to get Da's attention while he was in deep conversation with Mammy at the dining table nearby.

I spoke in a low voice, pointing to Iona, 'Da, Da, look at this.'

I tried twice to speak to him until Da eventually turned around to look.

He politely interrupted Mammy, 'Excuse me a minute.' He laid his knife and fork down and called out, 'Iona! Iona!'

No response.

All hell broke loose. Da jumped over to Iona then shouted to Mammy who, by this time, was standing with both hands covering her eyes.

'Get help!' he yelled. 'Get down to the police box and find someone. Get the police, a doctor, get someone!'

Mammy ushered me through to the bedroom where we hurriedly put on shoes and coats, then ran as fast as we could to the next street where the red police box stood proudly. If it wasn't manned, the public could open a small compartment that held a black telephone. People only had to pick up the handset, no need to dial, because once it was off the hook, it rang at the local police station. Mammy was apprehensive because she'd never used a telephone before. She opened the door and picked up the handset but put it down immediately without saying a word. I stood watching her as she wrung her hands.

Fortunately, a minute later, a young policeman arrived on his bicycle and they exchanged a few words. He asked Mammy who her doctor was as he was unlocking the main door of the police box, then dialled a number from another phone inside. After speaking quietly into the handset for a few seconds, he asked Mammy her address and relayed the information to someone at the station. He told her the doctor would be on his way shortly. Mammy couldn't speak, so the policeman focused on me, asking my mammy and da's names and about Iona, where we lived, what school I went to and what my da's job was. It seemed an eternity before the policeman looked at his pocket watch.

'OK, I think we could saunter back round.' He locked the door and put his hat back on. 'Would you recognise the doctor's car if it was sitting outside?'

'Yes,' Mammy managed a feeble reply.

Once we turned the corner to our flat, she pointed directly to the black Ford Anglia sitting outside number twenty-one and nodded her head. Then Mammy turned to the policeman, her face chalk white.

'I don't think I can go up.'

I looked up at his black-rimmed glasses and his strange hat.

'Let's go up the stairs as far as the door. I'll go in first, then come and tell you what's happening. Then you can decide.'

He did as he promised and left us standing outside the flat door, on the stairs where I had sat in fear with Iona only months before. None of us spoke until the policeman reappeared; he nodded and took us both inside. Complete with a stethoscope round his neck, the doctor was standing beside Da and Iona was sleeping on the couch. It transpired she had choked on a piece of orange. Da told Mammy he had put his finger down Iona's throat and she'd brought up the slimy piece of orange. I had been within seconds of losing another sister.

Although I didn't entirely know what dying was, the number of adults involved and the atmosphere in the house told me it wasn't a good thing to happen. That brought an end to us sitting alone with food, and I went through a spell of not wanting to go into the bed settee where Iona and I slept together. I was shaking. Neither Mammy nor Da asked me what the problem was, and I was too young to articulate my feelings. It was simply that I worried this dying thing might happen again when I was alone with my little sister. A relative calm developed in Mammy and Da for a while, as the near heartbreak stunned them.

By the time Iona was three, I could take her outside on my own. We played in the backcourts, the communal areas behind blocks of flats where women hung out their washing and kept the rubbish bins of coal ash and other debris. We tried to climb high walls and devised theatre shows with a few local children. It was normally an empty stomach that drove us home, but there was no way of knowing what we might find once we climbed the two flights of stairs. If Da wasn't home, we would have to stay hungry for a while longer. If he was there, food would be ready, but a quiet or tense atmosphere might overshadow our meal. A wrecked house came after the silence.

When things were peaceful though, we ate our meals in a convivial atmosphere and Mammy and Da told us bedtime stories which I particularly enjoyed. Eventually, the usual Goldilocks and the Three Bears type of tale began to drag, so Da recounted anecdotes about the war.

Iona fell asleep through boredom, but I listened intently. The stories involved soldiers marching or crossing rivers and became more interesting when I learned how the men had to face loss and trauma.

During the war, Da had been an ambulance driver, but he described his job as much more than that of a medic. Throughout these accounts, he portrayed himself as a hero.

'Now, these are secret stories. No one has ever to know that I was a special soldier. We called it the SBS, Secret Boat Service.'

That meant nothing to me. I never thought for a minute he might have embellished his tales to give himself a sense of importance; I felt the truth was in there somewhere about Da being more than an ordinary soldier. Like most children's fathers, he was a hero, in my eyes anyway.

What he didn't tell me until years later was that he had seen unbelievable casualties of war, some experiences he could never talk about: the brutality he witnessed between soldiers, the fear of bombing and shelling and the relentless wondering if he would ever see his family again. The twisted and torn bodies, severed limbs and men screaming in pain constantly haunted him and the loss of the few fellow soldiers he had befriended was immeasurable.

He recounted the story of his dearest friend, Archie, who was also a born-again Christian and part of a tank crew. He had lost his life, but not in the heat of battle. Archie was alone in the tank with the turret open when some form of artillery was fired, causing the lid to close and trap him. A fire was burning inside the tank. The other soldiers, including Da, could hear his horrific screaming, but there was nothing they could do. The commanding officer knew there was no escape but coaxed Archie to look out of the turret view port. At that, he raised his pistol and shot Archie between the eyes. It was the only way to end the torturous screams of a nineteen-year-old soldier who was never going to survive. Da was also tormented by the rapes and murders he saw and heard of in the small towns they marched or drove through. Some atrocities he managed to completely block out but he knew the brutality of war he had seen as an inexperienced man, not even in his twenties, would haunt him for the rest of his life.

His personal battle with Mammy took over, and he did what he thought was the best way to protect and care for his family,

In the summer, families flocked to the Scottish lochs to have picnics, play on the shore or sail in the clear water, and our family was no exception. When times were good, we spent holidays and days out together visiting attractive coastal villages along the River Clyde, loch-side campsites and the small islands off the west coast.

Along with Iona, I collected seashells and learned about the countryside. Even when our trips started well, however, they could develop at rocket speed into catastrophe. Fortnight-long camping trips were over in a matter of days if arguments started between Mammy and Da. Without warning, we could find him dismantling the tent, and there was absolutely nothing that could be said or done to stop him from his task of packing up every item. Disappointment flooded through me and Iona as we made our way home on the long bus journey.

On a short camping trip, Da drove a hired car to a beauty spot near Loch Long where we enjoyed a picnic, then he rented a rowing boat for the four of us. We set out from the shore, and Da took control of the oars.

At one point, Mammy looked down through the clear water and pointed to the rocks appearing below the surface.

'Look, I know what I'm doing. We're not in any danger,' he snarled.

He reminded her that he was in charge. But the rocks rose higher and the boat became stuck. I heard Iona begin to hum, a clear indication that she was anxious and would soon burst out crying.

'Can we take off our shoes and paddle to the shore?' I asked my da.

'No,' he answered, shaking his head. 'It's far too deep.'

I squeezed my eyes shut and Iona, still humming, cuddled into Mammy. Pushing the oars against the rocks only made things worse, and the stern remained wedged between two craggy boulders, while the strength of the lapping waves prevented the boat from breaking free. I dared to open one eye and looked into the deep water.

We're going to drown, I thought.

There was more than that to contend with. Da was mad because Mammy had been right. She was mad because he hadn't listened. In the end, he had to stand up and, balanced precariously, put one bare foot against a rock to manoeuvre us away.

No one spoke on the way back to the shore or in the car on the journey home the following day. My stomach tightened; I wanted to be home. Iona fell asleep.

The late afternoon traffic was building up in the city's direction and I could tell by Da's face that the slow pace exacerbated his bad mood. He remained totally silent, then saw an opportunity to overtake. At that, he headed into the empty lane for oncoming traffic. Driving silently and at speed past the almost stationary vehicles at his side, Mammy's screaming interrupted his thoughts.

'Adam Eden!'

With a shake of his head, he was back to the present and, roused from my dreamy state, I sat up straight in the back seat in time to see a car coming directly towards us. Da swerved at the last minute and the other car passed without incident. He had been so angry that he had put his family in danger and, without the safety of seat belts, we could have been wiped out in seconds.

Money was tight for working-class people in the 1960s. New furniture and household goods were things families had to wait for; food and clothing took priority. Little was available by way of legal credit and so working-class people had to save up for luxuries.

In the building where we lived, there were eight one-bedroomed flats but few children. For a few years, we were the only children living 'up the close', the flats above the ground floor. The entrances to the flats were clean and tidy, with a well-kept stairway. A couple, Jessie and Dick, lived on the top floor above us and acted like an aunt and uncle to Iona and me, encouraging us to visit for treats. Like the other neighbours, they had heard the commotions that went on between Mammy and Da but, unlike the others, they were polite and passed the time of day with our family. We girls never got involved with anyone else who lived up the close.

One Thursday morning during the summer holidays, Iona and I were visiting Jessie; Mammy was busy tidying up our flat when the doorbell rang. Expecting it to be us on the landing, she was taken aback to see two workmen in boiler suits standing in front of her.

'We've come to install your new fireplace.'

'Oh really? This is news to me. And which company are you from?'

They mentioned their company name, but Mammy took little notice because she certainly wasn't expecting a fireplace.

They confirmed her flat was second floor, right-hand side. One man consulted his notebook and told her that her husband had been in their showroom the week before and made the deal. It was not only done and dusted but also paid for; we were to have a new fireplace fitted.

'Our boss told us Thursday was the best day to install it. Is everything all right?'

She hid her confusion when they said they had to survey what was already in place and decide how to proceed with the job. After she asked them what it would look like, they showed her a picture of a marble fireplace. She let them in.

They set about demolishing the old, tiled fireplace and, by late afternoon, had replaced it with a splendid white one. The overhanging mantle top was something that Mammy had always craved; a place to display her special ornaments and a framed photograph of us that hadn't yet been destroyed.

Mammy dressed nicer than usual as she prepared for Da to come home; she made his favourite broth and even sent me to the corner shop to buy a tin of peas to complement the carrots that adorned the roast beef and potatoes. She looked classy by the time he arrived and told me she couldn't wait to hear what he had to say.

Da stopped abruptly as he came through the living room door and stared at the oversized fireplace now dominating the room. She expected a comment from him about the job being done on time as promised or the quality of the workmanship, but all he did was bite his bottom lip and breathe in sharply. His reaction was certainly not what she was expecting. They were both confused, and neither knew how to approach the situation.

For someone who had ordered and paid for a fancy fireplace to surprise her, he was acting remarkably disappointed. Then the sucking in of his lips told us all something was wrong. Da glanced from the fire in the fireplace to the photo on the mantlepiece, to the brass coal scuttle and back again to the fire.

He almost croaked, 'So, what's all this?'

Mammy tilted her head. 'You should know, you asked for it!'

He looked around the rest of the living room with saucer eyes, fearing that the fireplace might not be the only addition and calculating the cost.

'We can talk about it later,' he said.

When the usual routines of the evening had finished with us tucked up in bed, the pair sat down in front of the fire. I was told of the outcome a while later, when I was old enough to know how to keep a secret.

In a strong but fearful tone, Da had nodded towards the new installation. 'OK, what's the story behind this?'

Mammy recounted everything that had happened and the workmen's words. Shaking his head, he categorically denied having ordered it and emphatically reminded her he couldn't have paid for such a luxury. Initially, neither of them believed the other, but within a short space of time, they knew each was at a loss. Mammy couldn't remember the company name. Maybe something like Addison.

They went to bed with jumbled thoughts. In the morning, Da suggested they wait; for what he didn't know, but that's all they could do. He imagined they would get a letter from the company, if not a visit.

Nothing happened until a couple of weeks later when Mammy was returning from the butcher's shop with sausages and half a pound of bacon. Two streets away from our flat she saw a parked van and immediately recognised the name on the side: Bartholomew Addison and Sons, the name the workmen had given her. She peered through screwed-up eyes; yes, that was the name. Why hadn't she remembered it before? Now she was in a dilemma, but she wouldn't rock any boats. She put her head down and scurried home as fast as she could.

A few days later, she was in the greengrocer's shop when she heard snippets of gossip and put things together. One of the wealthier families in another street had ordered a fireplace. It should have been installed the week before, but when they contacted the company to ask where it was, they were told it had already been fitted. After inviting the company owner to come and look for himself, he discovered the mistake. It became clear the men had mounted the fireplace at the wrong address and, after trying unsuccessfully to locate it, the company had to give the rightful customer a new one. All the boss could do was write off the lost fireplace. Da never investigated further and Mammy kept her mouth shut for once in her life.

By the 1960s, larger grocery stores appeared and small concerns, like dairies and greengrocers' shops, were all but disappearing. The fruit market offered discounts on produce for stores such as the Co-operatives (Co-ops) that could buy in bulk. Da, with limited storage and customers, couldn't buy more than his usual two or three small boxes; he didn't qualify for any discount and had to sell at a higher price to cover his costs. Although the shop lost some custom, it could still provide specialities like homemade jams and baking along with dairy products.

Sadly, that wasn't enough to keep Eden's Dairy afloat because religion also played a part in its downward spiral. Da never opened the shop on the Sabbath. The newsagent next door opened on a Sunday morning and sold rolls, along with Sunday newspapers. One Monday morning, Da saw an empty milk crate in the newsagent's doorway and, putting two and two together, he figured the owner had seen a niche. He had offered customers milk at the same time as they bought rolls. If the newsagent could sell milk on a Sunday, customers wouldn't always need to buy it on the Monday from the dairy. Da was losing more business.

At mealtimes, Iona was engrossed in her food while I heard my parents turning to shop talk. Most of it was over my head, especially when Da spoke unfamiliar words like overheads and competition. Not long afterwards, I heard the sadness in Da's voice when he came home and announced the shop was finished.

He realised his only option was to sell up and look for work within one of the grocery shop chains. He took a job with the Co-op. After a few months, he had proved his worth and was appointed assistant branch manager. Eventually, he moved around different locations to troubleshoot in failing branches.

Da was happy again at his work, but his marriage was up and down. He never knew what he would face at home when Mammy continued her tirades. The combination of different stresses made them ticking time bombs.

Chapter 7

While we Edens were living in our one-bedroomed flat, the city council brought out a new housing initiative. Once the oldest child in a household reached ten years of age, they could have their family living arrangements assessed. Although we lived in a nice area, the flat was inadequate for a family of four.

On the outskirts of Glasgow, council housing estates sprang up to meet growing demand. Modern flats with at least two bedrooms and a separate kitchen appeared; this was a woman's dream in that era. My parents put in an application form in April 1962. Da wasn't so sure about housing estates, but he thought he'd see what the council offered them.

He prepared for stock-taking at his Co-op branch when a phone call came in from the head office. The board of directors had a proposal. A college in Loughborough, England, had an advanced management course beginning in September 1962. Da's name was put forward. Later, he told me that initially he thought about what it would mean to spend a year away from the family and decided not to mention it to us immediately.

Around the same time as the course offer, there was a reply from the council. Mammy opened the letter. A flat was available on the same estate in the East End of Glasgow, where Aunt Jane and Uncle Jack now lived with their nine children, including Elizabeth. Around six years before, she had temporarily been my little sister. Mammy announced the news to me and Iona and all we could talk about was what we would have in our new bedroom. As far as we were concerned, we were moving, and likely soon.

Da came home from work that night to hear about the letter. He argued that if we waited another year, we would have enough money to buy a bigger flat in a more salubrious part of the city, but Mammy wanted at least to see the council flat.

Nobody spoke throughout supper and at one point, I saw Mammy's tears dripping onto the table. I'd never seen her weep like that before; no anger, only disappointment. I copied her and Iona copied me. We didn't know why we were crying, but our wailing eventually became too much for Da, who put his knife and fork down and put his hands on his hips. He gave in and the next day he sent a reply.

It was mid-May when Mammy and Da went alone to have a look. Da repeated he didn't like the area and made more excuses: too many big families living together and a gang culture. But Mammy couldn't see past the flat itself; it had features she had fantasised about, including a pulley in the kitchen instead of the living room. She took us girls to see it.

We skipped along as we made our way through unfamiliar streets and squealed when Mammy opened the door of the empty, bottom-floor flat. It seemed strange to run up the long hall, which invited us into the spacious living room. We opened the glass-panelled door leading to a balcony which had enough room for a table and a couple of stools. We would have a good-sized bedroom and single beds. The other bedroom had two windows looking out in different directions.

Da accepted the flat and signed the agreement to move at the end of June, giving us time to pack up and sell our flat. Mammy was happy but Da wasn't going to get the respectable address he had yearned for. He liked the idea of us going to a school with an excellent reputation and having his own property. After all, he was the assistant manager at the Co-op and felt he had earned the esteem associated with his position; a council housing estate didn't offer sufficient prestige.

Balancing his work and home situation took Da a few weeks. The removal was uppermost in his mind but, in quiet moments, he gave the course some serious thought. On one hand, he would be on full pay without the responsibility of working in the shop; on the other hand, he'd have to dispense with his pledge to support local missionary work. A year was a long time to be away from us and he wondered how Mammy would cope.

In time, he explained to me how he had arrived at his final decision. It suddenly came to him one afternoon on his tea break: *Let them have the house; let them have all of it, let them have it to themselves.* His thoughts were clear. He would accept the place on the management course and we could experience life on the housing estate.

Once the move had been made, Da told Mammy he'd been selected for the course; he was to leave within a matter of weeks. He reminded her he wouldn't be around to do repairs. He would take responsibility for the rent, but she could deal with, among everyday living costs, the electricity bills. They divided the money from the sale of their old flat between them and Mammy furnished our new place while Da kept his half of the proceeds. Then he left to start his course.

With no one to help Mammy, a new life as a single mother lay ahead. The way she looked at it, she was already the one who dealt with me and Iona. She cooked and cleaned; she didn't see that Da's absence would make much of a difference as long as she had enough money for us to survive.

Caught up in our new adventure, the move to the estate and Da's departure happened so close to one another that none of us fully appreciated what his leaving meant. At least I thought we might be able to leave some vegetables if we didn't like them without him refusing to let us leave the table. Mammy enrolled us at school and did her best to blend in.

The mission was a thirty-minute walk away, but we joined the congregation anyway. Mammy encouraged us to choose friends from the limited number of youngsters in the flock. Sadly, that didn't protect us from the wicked ways of the world. We made other friends, some from school and some who lived nearby. I became close to Irene, who lived on the first floor of the next block of flats with two brothers, an older sister and a baby girl of about a year. It was commonplace for children of my age to go into friends' flats to wait for them to come out to play. I didn't tell Mammy that in some flats I saw older brothers or sisters smoking while being cheeky to their parents; initially I was wide-eyed at the banter, knowing some of what I heard were *bad* words.

I came home one afternoon to find Mammy had invited another mother in for a cuppy. It was then that she began to get an insight into what went on in some of the surrounding flats and the neighbourhood in general. It didn't take long for her to pick out the people she preferred us to mix with. She was disappointed when I told her Irene's dad seemed to sit around doing nothing while her mum cooked in a messy kitchen.

Irene's flat was bigger than ours. When I went to the door for her, I gathered the house rule was to close the bedroom door opposite the front door before opening it to anyone. One day I got as far as the broken mini chandelier that hung precariously from the hall light fitting. I never saw it lit. The bedroom door hadn't closed properly and I spied bikes piled on top of one another and the rest of the room in complete disarray. The stained bare floorboards could hardly be seen because of bags of boxes with clothes and bike tyres spilling out. What surprised me was the double bed in the middle of the chaos. I still don't know how her mum and dad got through the debris to climb in.

Worse still was the first time I was invited further into the flat. My sandals were sticking to the carpets. I walked in to see Irene's mum sinking into a black leather couch. There were no complete armchairs, the cushions were either removed or so thin they were practically non-existent. She was reading a paper and beside her, but a foot away, lay a sleeping one-year-old baby. Next to the little one on the couch was a fried egg; a strange scene.

One Friday, I went into Irene's living room to see her mum and dad looking stunned. He had apparently lost his pay packet as he had cycled home after work. Naïve as I was, I watched the reactions of both and concluded that Irene's dad wasn't in the least bothered; I felt he was lying. He knew exactly where his pay packet was. His wife, in tears, bleated on about how she wouldn't be able to feed the family. He sat smiling.

Here was a poor family with children ranging in age from one to eighteen. There was no sign of a bed in the room Irene and her sister slept in. I couldn't fathom it out but I guess the pile of blankets and cushions would have served as a place to lay their heads.

When I relayed my story to Mammy, she shook her head. I knew she felt sorry for them.

'This is not good. I can't help them and they're not the only family living like that. But you and Iona shouldn't be seeing this. I don't know if we've done the right thing coming here.'

Other things went on. One dark night, Mammy looked out the bedroom window at the local Co-op which was lit up only by the street lamp outside. She called me over and we stood for five minutes watching a boy of around nine. He had used a glass cutter to remove a section of the plate-glass window and was filling two enormous shopping bags with items from the display. We were stunned at his bravado and agreed his family would likely be waiting with knives and forks at the ready. Da, being a grocer, had told us that window displays were normally dummy containers like chocolate boxes filled with blocks of wood. Depending on what the boy's family found inside the stolen tins; they might have been sorely disappointed.

The break-in was a typical example of criminal behaviour on the housing estate and a reminder of how young children were trained and encouraged to be part of it. Mammy, now with an eleven-year-old and a five-year-old, was left to be our protector in this environment, which was alien to us all.

Soon after Iona had started her new school, as Da had predicted, suspicious conduct infiltrated our family. Within a few weeks, she came home with insignificant items which didn't belong to her. A green pencil she apparently found in the school corridor, a storybook and then a brown pencil case.

As the months went by, there were signs our new environment affected both Iona and me. Although we were pleased that our strict father was out of the picture, I knew Mammy was struggling and her moods swung between being full of fun to despondency. There wasn't any stability and Iona had ongoing nightmares where she dreamt of being lost and not being able to find her way home because a giraffe was holding her hand.

I got myself into childish disagreements. When asked in the playground to decide who I liked best between Elvis Presley and Cliff Richard; I was torn but had to make a rapid choice.

'Come on, Alice!' The blondie who had instigated the conversation put her hands up in the air.

'Choose one,' someone else said as I sidled nearer to Irene.

I chose Cliff and now, as part of the 'Cliff gang', they expected me to gravitate to their corner of the playground. Irene had followed my lead, which was a blessing, but the choice eventually had nothing to do with the two artists. It was all about the older, stronger characters creating division between the girls in the class.

Eve, from the Elvis group, challenged me to a fight because she didn't like me. After school, we walked through the estate with our respective gangs and I turned around to look behind; it was as though the entire school was following us. The masses were no longer interested in Elvis or Cliff, but in me and Eve.

On a slight incline leading away from the main street, Eve suddenly turned around and gave me a hard slap that I hadn't expected. I was embarrassed and humiliated and didn't retaliate. Her group burst out laughing, then disappeared to deal with some other petty incident.

But, through the living room window, Mammy had spied me surrounded by girls of all ages walking towards home. The questions started as soon as I walked through the door.

'What was all that about? Why the big gang of people with you in the middle?'

Although I was still shaking in my boots, I denied it had anything to do with me; Mammy didn't look convinced. She left well alone but reminded me of Da's concerns about gangs and fights.

It was difficult for eleven-year-old girls like me not to succumb to peer pressure and get up to mischief. Out in groups and stealing a bar of chocolate from the newsagents was commonplace. Worse still, the boys on the estate thought nothing of throwing a brick at a passing cyclist or demolishing workmen's huts.

Phone booths had a paper telephone directory lying on their shelves with lists of private numbers; that was tempting for the older teenagers who learned how to circumvent the pay process by tapping out the numbers like a Morse code. With the right touch and the correct pauses, these knowledgeable youngsters could call anywhere in Scotland for free, to the annoyance of the recipients of the calls.

A long-established pastime was to dial 999 and lie to the fire department that flames were leaping from a tenement block window. Within minutes, red fire engines screamed in the distance and those who had made the call ran and hid. The others hung around and shouted abuse at the heavily uniformed men, chucking stones and rotten food at the firemen. Even if there was a fire, groups hung around to throw objects at the men, stopping them from doing their jobs.

Teenagers emulated older brothers and sisters who smoked. Cigarettes were easy to find if parents left open packets lying around. I saw the adulation the teenagers received as they stood there, imitating film stars, waving their cigarettes between two fingers and blowing smoke rings into the air.

Alcohol was something completely different. Although the odd leftover can of beer would have been within reach for a lot of teenagers, it scared the younger ones when they saw drunken men in the street muttering incomprehensible words while drunken women shouted after them.

Mammy heard of stabbings and neighbours receiving prison sentences for fighting. Gangs with inflated egos weren't uncommon and, along with that, came a pack mentality. She heard that men in their late teens and early twenties found Dutch courage when they carried hammers, flick knives or sharpened steel combs. The challenge was always there from rival gang members wielding broken bottles or other deadly weapons and yelling out their gang name like a war cry. Unfortunately, there was a certain amount of respect for those with visible face or arm scars; they had a reputation to live up to every weekend.

Almost a year after our move, I started secondary school, where talk of sex was commonplace. A fourteen-year-old girl had just come back to school after giving birth to a baby boy. Some pupils were in awe of the mother because here was a girl, not much older than those in my class, who had given birth. It was a scandal.

The gossip filtered through the community and I confirmed the story when Mammy asked me about it. That was the icing on the cake when she told Da on his monthly weekend home. They knew the life we were being exposed to was a dangerous one and could have implications for our future if we got involved in crime and/or unwanted pregnancies.

The estate was breeding rough children. Da told me they had probably made the wrong choice with the housing estate; that our lives could be ruined before we were out of our teens.

Now the proud owner of an advanced management certificate, Da could more or less pick which branch of the Co-op he wanted to work in and enjoy a pay rise. Mammy told him she had had enough and finally agreed to move out of the estate. They were now looking for a more acceptable address and a new mission; something that gave them both a focus.

However, Da wondered if the damage had been done, if the rot had set in. His daily prayers included me and Iona. It was as though he was begging for us not to be harmed but, at almost twelve, I wasn't oblivious to something just as destructive, the battle cries and destruction from what should have been our paradise between four walls.

My parents looked for a two-bedroomed flat closer to the city centre and tried to be a happy family again. Without a car, there needed to be a place of worship within walking distance. Their ideal flat eventually came on the market, so they had a look at the surrounding area and saw the well-kept tenement buildings, a good-sized established park and a library. Schools were nearby. Da looked again at the asking price and made an appointment to view.

Unfortunately, there was only a church rather than a mission in the neighbourhood and it niggled Da that our religious education might be lacking. He felt the established church was failing to follow the scriptures and that fundamental Christian ideas were being overtaken by a lax approach to worshipping God. He pointed out that scripturally, women should have their heads covered when worshipping, but he had seen women walking into the church without a hat. In regular churches, it had also become acceptable for people to drop a sixpence or even threepence into the collection plate. Da could point out where the scriptures showed a tithe, a tenth, of income was the acceptable way to sustain the Lord's work.

The sellers of the flat, Mr and Mrs Smith, a childless couple in their late twenties, showed us around. Da's questions about their leaving the flat were met with weak smiles from Mr Smith. He said they hadn't been in the flat long, but now needed to move to England to be nearer to their aging parents. They shook hands on the price and the property deeds were signed. Despite Da's request, the couple never left a forwarding address for any mail that might arrive. And then we moved in.

Two floors up, double storm doors opened to reveal a small vestibule where the main door, complete with a stained-glass window, led into a square-shaped hall. From there, beautifully carved wooden doors led to two bedrooms, a good-sized bathroom, a cupboard, and a living room with a small kitchenette extension. The dated decoration screamed out, 'Room for improvement'. Da knew he was more than capable of making alterations to turn it into a dream flat. The washing green in the backcourt was ours every Wednesday – too bad if it rained on Mammy's wash day. Three or four unlocked wash houses leaned against a back wall. With deep double sinks and washing boards, they were still usable. But few women up the close ventured into the darkness behind the small-paned windows. That would have let the others know they didn't have a washing machine or a wringer at home. Nobody bothered about fixing the slates on the wash houses' roofs, so on rainy days, the plip-plop of raindrops echoed off the stained, unmanned sinks.

Two days after we moved, I celebrated my twelfth birthday with a meagre excuse for a birthday present because nobody was organised. The Lego was meant for a much younger child and the book on horses had clearly been chosen by Iona; I wasn't the least interested in animals. We were more settled by the time Iona turned six the following month. So life began again; new schools, new friends and a new place of worship.

Not long after we moved in, newspapers reported police were hunting for a gang who had perpetrated a robbery in England a few months previously. What sparked the public's interest was the involvement of an innocent man who had been forced to assist in what was eventually named The Great Train Robbery. Normally, an event like that in England would have been of limited significance to the people of Scotland, but the mail train had been travelling from Glasgow to London. Authorities worked on a valuable lead that some of the gang members were still in the Glasgow area. Da wasn't certain, but the man whose photograph appeared in the newspaper vaguely resembled Mr Smith. One evening, I overheard a serious conversation Mammy and Da had about it, but he decided it wouldn't be worth making waves. He wasn't convinced it was the same man, didn't want to waste police time, nor did he want to clype on a gang of dangerous men. He left well alone.

Despite Da doing most of the work in the flat by himself, money became tight as they forged ahead with alterations to the bathroom and kitchenette. We could say goodbye to holidays. There just wasn't enough money to go around.

But some things didn't change. Mammy said Da treated her as though she was stupid and ignorant. If a job like wallpapering or painting needed doing, she listened to his instructions, but often he would leave out essential information. Then he would shake his head.

'How did you do that?' he would say, holding up the torn wallpaper.

'You're not holding the wood right!' he snarled as he tried to hammer in a nail.

He would tighten screws then ridicule her because she couldn't loosen them. She got angry when he pointed out her mistakes, but she didn't destroy the flat or our possessions anymore; she valued the newness of it all. Also, she tried to fix what she could when things fell apart. Without the proper knowledge, she took a while to figure out how they could be repaired, but she did it. She might have made a better carpenter than Da.

What he didn't realise was that Mammy was a woman on the cusp of becoming independent. She could do a lot; the only thing she couldn't do was to move away from her unhappy family life because she didn't have a regular income. She didn't differ from many other women in that respect. She sometimes voiced her thoughts and wondered if things would ever change financially and go in her favour so that she could break free.

Leaving was impossible, so giving Da the silent treatment became her new way of dealing with irritation.

On the day we had moved in, Mammy stowed small boxes in a window seat under a bay window. They put three suitcases filled with surplus bits and pieces at the back of the hall cupboard. In time, we joined forces in retrieving the suitcases. Da needed the cupboard emptied because he hoped to create new cupboards the length of the hall.

It seemed like Christmas all over again as we put the suitcases in the middle of the living room floor. Iona and I pulled out old dolls and a few knick-knacks that now meant very little to us. Mammy and Da retreated to the hall to discuss the soon-to-be new cupboards. Their conversation was of no interest to us; we didn't know about rulers, hammers and chisels.

When I walked through the hall, I saw a duffle bag, like a backpack, on the floor.

'Whose is that?' I asked.

'It isn't ours. They've left it behind. Looks like it's full of old clothes. We'll have to contact the people who lived in the flat before us,' Da replied.

And that was the end of the matter as far as I was concerned. My parents knew best and they would deal with it.

At half-past eight, they herded us off to bed. Many months later, Da told me about that night. He and Mammy had sat beside the dying embers of the fire. When he put two more coals on, he saw her surprise. That was usually her job. But he had something to discuss and needed her to be calm. He suggested they have a cuppy.

Da volunteered. 'Let me check on the girls while you put the kettle on.'

I remember him coming in. He knew Iona was sleeping when he removed her askew glasses and she didn't stir. He gently prised the latest book on caring for dogs from her hand and placed it on the floor. I was pretending to be asleep, but thankfully Da never suspected I could be as devious; he surveyed my curled-up body and my face half-buried into my pillow. Once he had gone, I brought out a tiny torch and the latest teen magazine my friend Michelle had lent me.

Da had sat back in his fireside chair.

'I have to tell you that my mother isn't very well. I got word that she's been diagnosed with a heart condition and I'm worried about her,' he said.

Mammy hadn't seen my grandma, Agnes, for years. The way things were between Mammy and Da, it worked out best if he visited his family alone. In the past, she'd never been able to do more than pass unsavoury remarks to him after they'd visited. Old Rob, my grandad, had a thick Irish accent, so we couldn't understand a word. Other than a quick hello, nothing more was said between us as he sat quietly in his chair. Grandma was a peaceful, obedient wife who never questioned her husband's wishes. Old Rob referred to her as Mother. It irked Mammy that she obeyed his every command. Da knew his mother was a traditional woman; he also realised he had a different type of woman on his hands with Mammy.

Da said that he would visit his mother several times over the coming weeks. Then he changed the subject.

'Any idea where the duffle bag came from?'

'Not a clue, haven't seen it before. It must have been here when we moved in. Who put the suitcases in the cupboard?' Mammy asked.

'The removal men. I think they threw the cases in without even bothering to look. To be honest, even if I'd put them there, I wouldn't have seen a bag as small as that in a dark corner. I mean, there's no light in there yet.'

As an honest man, he felt he really should take steps to find whoever it belonged to. Apart from going to the police or the solicitor who had dealt with the sale of the flat, he didn't know where to start and asked himself if he should bother about some old duffle bag. Mammy filled me in on the full story of the bag after we had been in the flat for almost a year.

After that weekend had passed, and when everyone was out, she had inspected the bag.

He's going to fling that out, she thought as she shook her head.

Mammy thought we might use it. The contents probably weren't any good; she'd have to rummage through to have a good look. Retrieving it from the cupboard, she unbuckled it and emptied the contents onto the fireside rug.

The label on the ivory blouse showed it was a decent make. She held the long, checked skirt to her waist. It sat just above her ankles. The tan bag and shoes matched the light brown headscarf. She thought about keeping them for herself, but whoever had worn them had not been as rotund as she. When she stuck her hand right to the bottom, she felt something that made her squeal; she dropped the bag and jumped back. It had felt hairy, like an animal. With her hand covering her mouth, she waited a few seconds to make sure nothing moved. She got a wooden spoon from the kitchen and hesitantly poked around inside the bag. She was brave enough to pull the hairy thing out; it was a short, curly, light brown wig. Once Mammy had recovered from her bout of laughter, she surveyed the stash in front of her and folded the blouse, ready to put it back.

The sun streaming in the living room window struck the inside of the empty duffle bag; she told me she saw a slight bulge. After inspecting it, she found an extra piece of material sewn onto the lining; it was only because Mammy fancied herself as a seamstress that she spotted it. Someone had skilfully sewn it in, although the stitching differed slightly from the rest. She couldn't resist investigating and held her breath as she persevered to undo the end of the thread. After the wig, she said nothing would have frightened her.

She picked at the stitching until she could insert her thumb and forefinger, then pulled on a piece of brown paper. It was the edge of a sealed envelope. There wasn't any writing on the outside. Her heart was beating fast, and she licked her lips twice before taking the plunge. Mammy couldn't believe her eyes. Inside were some notes in different denominations. She held her breath and counted it, £50 in all. That was a substantial amount of money. Before she'd had time to think, her hand was back at the seam, feeling around.

A few minutes later, she had opened four brown envelopes and discovered something more interesting than a pile of worn clothes. She held onto £200. Mammy laughed as she told me she felt like a female version of the Count of Monte Cristo. The only time she'd seen a bigger amount was when they had sold their first flat and she and Da had split the money. She showed it to me.

'Look at that, you'll probably never see as much money again in your life!' She'd thrown nine £100 bundles from the top shelf of the wardrobe onto the bed.

Now here Mammy was, looking at another tidy sum and wondering what Da would say.

She thought about the time when her brother, Georgie, had sent her a share of the winnings from the horse racing and Da had stood over her while she flushed it away. That memory made her think she shouldn't bother telling him about this windfall, but she wondered how she could keep the £200 that lay in front of her. If she told him, no doubt he'd have some rebuff about it possibly being from a dishonest source and she could imagine it floating down the River Clyde. It was then she made her mind up. She'd never tell him; she'd put it somewhere safe and if he ever found it, she could honestly say that it must have been left by the previous owners. In the meantime, she had a stack of money in her possession, and that's where it was going to stay.

After double-checking the raincoat pockets and inside the handbag, Mammy was sure she had searched every nook and cranny. She replaced the clothes, buckled the duffle bag and put it back into the cupboard. Her task now was to find a good hiding place for the money.

Sadly, she didn't have enough to start a new life without Da. What she needed for that was a regular income. This unexpected gift would have to be spent.

Over the next few days, she thought of where she could keep the money safe. After a few unsuccessful ideas, she finally hit on one that would replicate the original hiding place. She found a beige handbag that had enough room to make a false lining and set to work to create a secret compartment for the £200. The only remaining problem was how to spend it. New items for the house were out of the question. The odd pair of stockings for herself or underwear for me or Iona would be OK. The money had to be spent on things that no one would notice or question.

Each Friday over the next few months, Mammy took the bus into the city centre. Starting with upmarket department stores, she sauntered in and paid over the top for a good lipstick and a decent hairbrush; the shop assistants didn't flinch at the £5 notes. Then, as she became bolder, she built up a collection of secret purchases: silk scarves, leather gloves and expensive corsets. She was careful never to buy more than one of any item at a time and always threw out something similar in her existing meagre collection. Through time, Mammy owned items that most women of her social standing could only dream of, but she never revealed their true value to anyone who passed a comment on how smart she looked. What they thought was a fake pearl necklace had cost an arm and a leg.

Eventually, Da decided to paint the inside of the hall cupboard where he once again came across the duffle bag of leftover clothes. He said there was no point in keeping them and wanted to bin them. Mammy agreed but suggested they keep the bag; after all, it might come in handy if us girls went on a school trip. Once the clothes were disposed of, Mammy had given a wry smile. She was indeed a fortunate woman to have taken the time to inspect the bag; the source of her now irreplaceable wardrobe and fabulous days out.

It surprised her at how easy it was to dispose of the cash, especially when she found that with the proper attire, she was welcomed into upscale restaurants to enjoy afternoon tea while reading *Woman* magazines. There was even a generous tip for the immaculately dressed waitresses. When she recounted her escapades to me, her face lit up with delight.

'That's what's missing,' she had mumbled one Friday afternoon in the George Hotel. She looked around at the couples and groups of three or four ladies. Although she didn't mind being alone, there would have been something pleasant about meeting a friend and having someone to chat to while waiting for the plates of scones and fresh cream cakes to arrive.

In another city centre hotel lounge the following week, she spied a woman sitting alone at a corner table sipping tea from a china cup. Mammy reckoned she must have been waiting for someone. She kept a surreptitious eye on the woman and let her mind take in what she was seeing. That's what my mammy wanted to look like. The woman would have been near Mammy's age and dressed appropriately for the occasion, wearing expensive attire. The flouncy collar on her cream blouse gathered at the neck to form a neat bow and showed off her voluptuous figure. With a navy, calf-length skirt, she was the picture of glamour. The glimpse Mammy got of her black-patent shoes showed they teamed up with the exquisite handbag slung over the back of her chair.

'That's also what I'm missing,' Mammy had muttered as the waitress arrived with a china teapot and matching pot of hot water.

'I beg your pardon, ma'am?' she enquired.

'Oh, I'm so sorry, my dear. My mistake. I thought I was missing something, but here it is!' Mammy replied, holding up a silver teaspoon.

What made her sit back abruptly in her seat was not so much that she had caught herself mumbling, but the voice that had come out of her mouth. She had used a tone and accent that she'd only witnessed from the glamourous stars in the few films she had seen: Bette Davis, Rita Hayworth or Ingrid Bergman. Mammy smiled; she had used a posh voice; she had got away with it and it hadn't been so difficult. With a bit of practice, her posh voice became her normal voice as soon as the spick-and-span concierges opened the doors of tea-rooms and restaurants. If she chose a table on the upper floor with a view of the city, that meant a ride in an elevator with the uniformed porter who accompanied her to her destination. How invigorated Mammy felt, knowing she was free on Fridays when she sent us to school dinners.

In December 1964, Da came into my bedroom one morning and woke me. He told me my grandma had passed away. It took me a moment to process what was happening. I thought I was dreaming when I heard his next words.

'Always remember this, Alice; your mother is the most important person in your life.'

He held a silver 6d in the palm of his hand. I put my hand out to take it, thinking I was getting some extra pocket money. Da quickly closed his hand over the coin.

'This was in Grandma's apron pocket when she died.' His mother's coin was special to him and he kept it for the rest of his life. He treasured the 6d and Mammy treasured her £200.

Old Rob couldn't live without his wife and went to meet his Maker three months later in February 1965. Their house sold quickly, and the proceeds split between Da and his three siblings. He never shared a penny.

Relative calm had descended as jobs in the flat distracted Mammy and Da but there was always a cloud hanging over me as I waited for disruption of some sort to start.

Chapter 8

We joined groups at the church. I enjoyed Brownies and Guides, but Iona took longer to settle and school was as far as she got. As a baby, she had been anxious if anyone other than Mammy was pushing her pram and her insecurity was coming to the forefront again. She wouldn't go out to play unless I was there. At seven years old, she wanted to play with skipping ropes or a couple of hand balls, too babyish for me. She couldn't keep up with our group of twelve- and thirteen-year-olds who played hide and seek or played marbles in the middle of the road until someone shouted, 'Car!' As young teenagers, we were becoming conscious of each other. Hair and fashion obsessed some girls while the boys tried to be macho.

I found my patience fraying with the younger boys, who were bothering us girls when we tried to have private, girly discussions while leaning against the lampposts. One day, a boy who lived nearby hit me on the arm, then grabbed the comic I was holding before he ran away. I gave chase but couldn't quite catch up, although he was within striking distance. To make sure I got him back, I stretched my arm out and pushed him forward while he was darting along at full speed. He landed flat on his face and ran home screaming. I also went home because I thought there might be some backlash from his older sibling. Within five minutes, the boy and his mother were at our door. Da called me from my bedroom and asked if I was responsible. It looked as though a gang of hooligans had beaten the boy up.

'Yes, because he hit me and took my comic. But I only pushed him.'

Even I knew that grabbing a comic didn't justify the mess the boy was in. Da's face fell and I could tell he didn't know how to deal with the situation. This wasn't a suitable environment for his girls. Iona was lonely, and I was wild.

Other factors were coming into play. Da was restless because there wasn't a mission nearby, and Mammy found it increasingly difficult to haul bags of shopping for a growing family up two flights of stairs. Something had to be done and after a year in the flat, Da heard news of an overspill scheme that encouraged families to move out of the city and into one of five new towns. If the man of the house secured a job, the family could apply to move. The council would provide a house rent-free for a year to encourage incomers.

This time, Da made sure he had Mammy's attention when he read out the details on the paperwork, named the new towns, and spoke about the pros and cons of each. They selected a town on the east coast of Scotland, thirty miles from Glasgow, and put in the housing application. At the same time, Da completed the paperwork to transfer from one branch of the Co-op to another. It was accepted immediately. There were two choices of areas within the town. The first was where most of the overspill families from the city went. New two- and three-bedroomed flats were being filled daily. The second possibility was at the other side of town, an older house with back and front gardens and next to a river. Having experienced the housing estate, it didn't take long for my parents to plump for the latter. They packed up, sold their flat and left the city.

I saw Mammy was clinging to her beige handbag for dear life as we travelled to meet the removers at the new house. By that time, she had told me she had a wee bit of money left. But this was our secret.

Number twenty-two Burns Road had two bedrooms and a bathroom upstairs with a living room and a spacious kitchen downstairs. One of the last things Mammy did with her dwindling find from the duffle bag was to buy bikes for us girls. We were about to experience something different from city living. As soon as we enrolled in our new schools, for the third time within two years, we donned new school uniforms and joined a new set of friends.

With a change of house and two growing girls, choices often had to be made about who got what by way of clothes. I dreaded coming home to discover that Mammy had found a bargain. The day she presented me with clumpy school shoes guaranteed to last for years, there were tears in my eyes. Mammy tried to convince me they were perfect for the coming winter.

'What else are you going to wear, Alice? Your other shoes are letting in water.'

The next morning, it was raining and I had no choice but to wear the dreaded shoes to school. I wondered what my classmates would have to say. Nobody mentioned the shoes in the line going in or inside the classroom. At break-time, I tucked my feet under a bench to hide the half-price Tuf shoes meant for boys, but the other girls had been whispering and spoke out.

'Are you hiding your new shoes from us, Alice?'

I bluffed my way through my embarrassment and placed my feet in full view of everyone, answering with pride, 'No, why would I be hiding them?'

But inside I was humiliated. Of course I was hiding them. No matter what, it was important to at least try to be like the other girls. It was another blow to my dwindling self-esteem.

Mammy wasn't too proud to bring some second-hand things into the house either. I was about the same height as the grown-up young lady next door, who would often send in a bag of clothes. She was of working age, so only a few items suited me; her womanly cast-offs were inappropriate, but my mammy persuaded me to wear the brown corduroy coat and the knee-length brown pleated skirt to our new mission. Once out of the house, I knew I was being watched.

I could practically hear the conversation from next door. 'Oh, doesn't that look nice on Alice?'

I was glad when Mammy saw my point; she agreed that the hand-me-downs were not what suited a younger girl and gave most to charity. The girls at school were showing an interest in make-up and clothes. On the weekends, they transformed themselves by replacing their school uniforms with knee-length boots and mini-skirts. It was a struggle for me because, even if I got something new, it was only ever semi-fashionable. Rather than pleading for something else, I lost interest in being a follower of fashion.

Iona was luckier, I was convinced of that. She had grown into a beautiful girl. Her longer-than-normal eyelashes framed her wide, grey-blue eyes. Even though her hair had never been allowed to grow back to its pigtail length, she suited how it now sat attractively on her shoulders. In company, people commented on how pretty she was.

She was more fashion-conscious than me. I often heard her reporting back to Mammy about what her friends were wearing and asking for the same. I saw that my younger sister had devised some cunning plans for new clothes and knew how to manipulate Mammy. She wasn't as successful with Da. When Iona asked him for branded or slip-on shoes, I heard her being told, 'Not now, maybe next month.'

Iona would come home the following day with a heel flapping off or the buckle ripped from her existing shoes. It worked; Mammy took her to get the much hankered-after latest style.

I was tired of making new friends in each new location. I tried my best to merge with existing groups, but my background of Bible stories, night-time prayers, and grace before meals set me apart. If a new friend ever called on me at home, Da kept up his habit of asking them what their surname was. He continued looking for Catholics. I remembered that in the city there had been a religious divide and Da would do his best to make sure it stayed that way, in our home at least.

Still, the house in the new town had a positive effect on us for a year. Mammy was calmly pottering in the garden as her mind focused on bedding plants and hedges. It was comforting for her to walk the half-hour into town along the banks of the river as she breathed deeper and felt at one with nature.

The Co-op promoted Da to shop manager. Once again, he became known for his meticulous stock-taking procedures. As grocers' shops expanded and commercial law allowed them to sell tobacco and spirits, Da had a problem.

When his boss said the company expected him to stock-take the alcohol, he didn't hesitate to tell them his religious principles wouldn't allow him to touch a single bottle. Da suggested they bring in a second manager for that job. That wasn't workable and so, without consulting Mammy, Da walked away from his post. His days in the grocery trade were over because of his profound religious convictions.

He secured a job as a caretaker at a sports centre and took a second job as a taxi driver when his hours permitted. The months passed and life revolved around the house, work and the mission. Eventually, he applied for a job as a bus driver and, although he had to work every second Sunday, he didn't see he had a choice. He was the breadwinner and, in his eyes, working now and again on the Sabbath was less of an evil than handling alcohol.

Sundays were still special days; days of rest. We liked Sundays because there was no school. Da didn't always go to work and there was more time in the morning to spend as a family before heading to the mission. Although we saw and heard arguments between our parents on weekdays, a Sunday tended to be quarrel-free. Our hair was usually washed the night before and, at thirteen, I got ready quickly. Seven-year-old Iona took ages picking out a special outfit. We would be neat and spotless by the time we left home for the half-hour walk to the eleven o'clock service.

Mammy also appeared happier at breakfast time on Sundays. No one was grabbing a last-minute plate of cornflakes before dashing out the door. There was time to show her culinary skills by preparing a spread for the family.

We didn't have a dining room, but there was enough space in the living room to set up the gate-leg table with four chairs and bring out the hand-embroidered tablecloth and napkins. We helped to set the table. No one commented when Iona mixed up the cutlery or put the side plates in the wrong place. Mammy and Da smiled and nodded knowingly at each other. I took charge of the matching milk jug and sugar bowl and Mammy carefully arranged the jam pot and butter dish. On a morning like this, we used our best crockery. It certainly became a feast for a king when the bacon, sausages and eggs appeared.

One Sunday, while we tucked into our scrumptious breakfast, Iona watched how Da ate his bacon, egg and toast. He cut them into small pieces, then speared a bit of each on his fork; she copied him. Mammy poured more tea just as Iona got something sticky on her fingers. She looked at her hands, then tried to clean her fingers by wiping them down the front of her dress.

Da saw this and in a harsh, scolding tone, he shouted, 'Don't do that, Iona. Don't wipe your hands on your clothes. That's what napkins are for!'

Iona's face crumpled, and she hung her head in shame. Mammy wanted to defend Iona but didn't quite know how to. Within minutes, Da had done the same; he had taken his hands and, without thinking, had run them down the front of his cardigan.

Mammy seized the moment and emulated his harsh, scolding manner. 'Don't do that, Adam. Don't wipe your hands on your clothes. That's what napkins are for!'

He didn't know how to respond. He had been caught out. We sat tense and silent. Something was brewing; Da was about to blow up.

It happened in a flash. Still seated, he put his hands on the rim of the table and suddenly lifted it upwards. It had moved about six inches when things slid to the edge. Iona turned to get off her chair, and Mammy grabbed her before a flying fried egg hit her Sunday frock. I realised the table wasn't only being hoisted up; it was being completely upturned, and I jumped back in time to avoid the jam dish that was heading in my direction. Da held the tablecloth in place for good measure so that butter, milk and sugar landed in an unceremonious heap on the floor. Dishes cracked as they hit each other, and shards of china bounced off the linoleum and embedded themselves in the rug. Bacon and eggs mixed with tomato sauce didn't look as appetising anymore.

As was the usual procedure when the house looked like a battlefield, nothing was said and Iona and I immediately obeyed Mammy when she told us to go upstairs and get our hats and coats. Once ready, we picked up our Bibles, stepped over the disarray on the floor and headed towards the back door. As a family, we walked down the road to the mission in near silence. We would deal with the chaos when we got home; the chaos of the ruined breakfast would be easier to fix than the chaos of our dysfunctional family life.

Once that particular argument had disappeared into the ether, several new things appeared after a period of calm: a radiogram, a rented television and a beige Mini, one of the most economical models on the market. The car was good news for Mammy as it meant help with the shopping, while the sources of entertainment were wonderful news for me and Iona. I was delighted with the record player inside the radiogram. Providing I could find songs that didn't include blasphemous words, I intended to spend my pocket money on records. Iona was glued to the television every day, watching things that weren't of any great interest, but she liked to commandeer the choice of programmes.

Early one evening after I had finished my homework, I sat down in front of the television shortly before six o'clock, happy to be on time for one of the few programmes I liked, *The Monkees*. Five minutes before it started, Da appeared from what he had been doing in the back garden and announced, 'I want to see the six o'clock news.'

This was the first time he'd ever let it be known he was interested in the news at that time; normally he waited until much later.

Thinking he was joking, I said, 'Ah, but my programme is about to start.'

'I'm watching the news and that's it.' His voice stronger than normal. 'Every time I come in here, the television is on and it's not me who's watching it. Either I watch the news or it's going off.'

I could tell I had rankled him, but I wondered why he had seized the moment to take his annoyance out on me, given that it was normally Iona who jumped up every two minutes to alternate between channels. *The Monkees* mattered to me; it would be the talking point at school the next day. Something was bubbling under the surface with Da and I was on the receiving end.

I stormed upstairs to the bedroom. The way he had addressed me was unusual, and I became more confused when, at six o'clock on the dot, rather than hearing the news coming on, I heard the music for *The Monkees*. I expected it to change any minute, but it didn't and my snatched thought of going downstairs dissolved when I heard raised voices; they were arguing again. He didn't watch the news, and I never got to see the programme. My da was the man of the house and I wouldn't have argued with him, but I wished we'd been able to negotiate or compromise.

Being at school with friends was a distraction from what was going on at home. In the main, I never had friends call at the house, but I could go to see them. Not only was it a chance to relax but also an opportunity to witness a different type of interaction between other parents. I saw harmony where some of my friends' parents appeared to involve their children in decision-making, even if it was only to explain why a certain rule was being implemented. No one clarified the rules in our home. Da's attitude was *do as I say* and that was that.

It annoyed Iona when Da put some stipulations in place for each second Sunday when he was working. We had to go to the mission as normal and the television was never to be on. While I wouldn't have gone against his wishes, Iona was different. She didn't see what harm it would do to have the television on, and besides, he would never know. One Sunday, while Da was working, Iona asked Mammy if she could watch a special wildlife programme. It took little persuading, but Mammy warned Iona that she could only watch the half-hour programme, then the television had to go off.

Two weeks later, when Da was working his Sunday shift, the same thing happened, but Iona told Mammy there was something more interesting coming on after the wildlife programme. She won and continued watching. That was the start of a bad habit.

As the Sundays went by, the pattern changed and the television would go on earlier and off later. More often than not, Mammy had to remind Iona to put the television off minutes before Da appeared from his shift. But if Mammy became absorbed in whatever she was doing in the kitchen, she forgot about Iona and her programmes.

It was all too much for me. I disappeared upstairs when the television was on; I didn't want to be involved in any more disobedience. With everyone in different rooms, Iona took control of the very thing Da had forbidden.

One Sunday evening around eight-thirty, Iona was doing the usual changing channels. For some reason, Da had finished work earlier than normal and managed to get a lift home. When he turned the corner in the semi-darkness, he looked over at the house. The flashing from the television would have been visible from outside through the finely woven living room curtains. Iona heard the back door open, jumped up from her seat and turned the television off – there weren't any remote controls in those days. She sat back down and continued to stare at the now blank screen, a real giveaway.

Da was furious. He walked over to the television set without taking his coat off, put his hand on the back of it and felt it warm. He took the plug out of its socket before getting his screwdriver and undoing it from the cable. No words were spoken; Iona went to bed after he started making sucking noises between his teeth. No doubt, his emotions were a mix of fury and disappointment. He would have known Mammy had allowed this against his wishes. She actively encouraged us to disobey him and, for all he knew, we had spent the afternoon and evening in front of the television. The action was not only a slight against him but also against God and the Sabbath.

The next morning, he was on an early shift and left before I got up. It was then I saw the plugless cable draped over the television and asked why. Mammy related the story. On my return from school, there was a gap where the television had been.

The only time I heard Da swear was shortly after this incident. He was angry with Mammy for allowing Iona to disobey him, so he laid down the law about other things. If we asked for some new item of clothing, he marched us upstairs and opened our wardrobe doors.

'Look at the amount of clothes you've got in there! You don't need any more.'

I had to be in at the times he specified. It didn't matter if there was a special event; there was no bending of the rules.

'I've said nine o'clock and I mean nine o'clock. Not a minute later.'

Mammy argued that he was making life difficult for me, at which point I saw him glare at her and heard him whisper, 'One day there'll be bloody murder in this house!'

There were secrets in our family, ones that Da kept from Mammy and vice versa. Some secrets were never meant to be discovered, while others were revealed at the perfect moment to create as much shock or disappointment as possible. It was all about mind games. Mammy accused Da of being secretive, so she was determined to be the same. The difference was she wanted him to find out she could be devious, while he didn't want anyone to discover his skeletons in the cupboard.

One example of a story he didn't want revealed involved Sheena Munro. When Da drove buses, the driver sat closed in at the front while a conductor or conductress dealt with the people coming on and off, taking fares and distributing tickets. The only contact the driver had with his conductor was at the beginning and end of their shift or, if there was time at a terminus, they might have a few minutes to chat before they made the return journey. Da had worked with a series of conductors and, at one point, he had a conductress, Sheena. At home, he never spoke about his work, so he didn't tell me then that he enjoyed working with her. As the male and the driver, he deemed himself to be the more important worker and felt it was natural for her to do things the way he wanted. It suited him to have a compliant, polite and attractive woman to work with. He was disappointed when Sheena's shifts were changed and he was given Jimmy Dawson as his conductor.

Working with other men meant Da usually had to listen to vulgarities and profanities not only in the canteen but also on break at the terminus. Over a few weeks, Jimmy shared his life story. It upset Da to think that Jimmy's wife was sitting at home with their child while he was spouting off stories about his lover. His new girlfriend had, unbelievably, moved into the family home, much to the displeasure of Jimmy's wife and the disgust of Da. The whole situation was alien to a man of God, but it wasn't Da's place to criticise and, to remove himself from the situation, he asked for a change of conductor and specifically the return of Sheena. His request was granted and, years later, he told me the story about the simple friendship he and Sheena had shared.

It had been a sunny day as Sheena's husband, Doug Munro, cycled home after visiting his mother. He saw a bus parked at the terminus near a quiet public garden, and two figures on the grass. It surprised him to see that the woman sitting down was Sheena. The other person lying on the grass, he presumed, was the bus driver. Doug was about to pull on the brakes so that he could stop and say hello when he saw the driver leisurely roll over onto his side and prop himself up on his elbow. He picked what looked like a tiny daisy and held it out to Sheena. To Doug, the two of them looked comfortable, but *he* wasn't. There was something about it that wasn't right. His wife was sitting with another man, albeit out in the open. Doug had never expected her to put herself in a situation that could be construed as inappropriate. It looked as though they had more than a working relationship. He kept cycling and decided to keep his swirling thoughts to himself.

The scene with Sheena sitting on the grass haunted Doug for days. Although he wasn't angry, he was confused and hurt. He tried to remember anything Sheena had said about the driver she was working with but couldn't. He brought the subject up a few days later and found out more than he had bargained for. Adam Eden, a God-fearing married man, had been prepared to change his shifts to team up with her. He took his holidays at the same time so that their work pattern wasn't interrupted.

Doug was a simple soul who had lived in the shadow of his older brother, Shug – a scoundrel known and feared by most, especially when he had a drink in him. Shug had a soft spot for Sheena; she could usually talk him out of a foul mood. Doug couldn't keep what he had witnessed to himself for long and told a speechless Shug, who growled and said he didn't like the sound of this Adam. Shug made it his mission to warn him off; he never trusted folk who came across as squeaky clean.

Days later, Mammy and Iona left to spend seven days at Butlin's Holiday Camp. A site in England had been taken over by a group of churches and missions for a week and was dedicated to Christian services for adults and children. There were amusements and rides for the young ones after the services. I had exams, so I stayed home with Da who was working an early shift that week.

On Thursday at lunchtime, he had been surprised when his boss called him in to say a letter had been handed into the bus depot. It was for someone called Adam Edan and his boss was sure it was for Da. Often, our surname was spelled wrong, and although he was used to it, the mistake truly irked him. He thanked his boss and apologised for any inconvenience; he couldn't figure out why or even how a letter had arrived at his place of work. He would wait until he was alone in a safe place to find out what all this was about. Da looked at his watch. He had very little time to eat, change his clothes and make his way to the mid-week meeting he was to host at six o'clock. He practically ran all the way home, hung his coat up, tore the envelope open and stuffed it in his pocket. Edan indeed! He unfolded the contents.

Sheena is part of my family, my HAPPY family. Get your hands off her. Get lost. Get different shifts from her or I'll change your life so that you'll wish your mother had never met your father. Big Shug.

He was catching his breath when he physically jumped at the back door opening.

Walking up the garden path, I had seen into the house through the living room windows and straight into the kitchen where I saw Da leaning against the doorpost, reading. I knew it was a letter because of the size of the page. After walking around the side of the house, I opened the back door. There hadn't been enough time for him to move position and I thought it strange to see him taking time to pull up his right sock. No letter was to be seen. He welcomed me as if he had been doing nothing else but standing at the kitchen door. Although I would never have asked him who the letter was from or what it was about, it made me wonder what could have been so much of a secret that he had reason to be furtive.

'Oh, Alice! Hello, I wasn't expecting to see you home so early.' His voice didn't betray him.

'I'm out early because my exam is finished.'

'I forgot.'

I wasn't sure if there was a sermon on the way and I couldn't figure out the scenario I had witnessed through the window, but it was better to leave well alone. If I dared to stay around, I might not get an answer, but he would trap me with quotes from the Bible and advice on how I could save my soul. I got up the stairs as quickly as my legs would carry me. Better to stay in the bedroom for a while. Da called up to ask if I would like some tea, but I said no. I was just about to go round to the local newsagents for a packet of crisps.

What I didn't know then was that once I had left, he pulled the letter from his sock and felt sick as he read it a second time. His life was being threatened by Big Shug.

He shook his head in disbelief and went into a sort of trance for a few seconds.

When I came back from the shop, Da noticed another envelope perched against the wooden clock on top of the long sideboard. He hadn't meant to bother with it at that precise moment, but before he was aware of what he was doing, he'd opened it while he was talking to me. This time, he pulled out a two-page letter.

J W Hastings and Sons, Bournemouth, England.

Dear Mr Eden,
Subject – Cash Investment.
We are dealing with the late Mr G Smith's estate and hope to tie it up promptly. We need evidence of all his assets before submitting the paperwork to the solicitors dealing with his estate.

He is survived by his wife, who has informed us that you knew something of his business dealings. We must trace and check his past and present properties and investments, which we understand have involved you since 1964.

We believe he sold you a property at Craigpark Street, Glasgow. We understand that payment and paperwork for the property were in order and completed according to the gentleman's agreement you made with Mr Smith. However, Mrs Smith tells us he also handed over £2,000 for you to invest on his behalf. Mrs Smith seeks knowledge of the capital and interest gained which, by now, if invested wisely, could be substantial.

Please contact our office either in writing or by telephone so that we can make the final adjustments to the late Mr Smith's estate.
With kindest regards,

Da showed me the scribbled signature. None of us could decipher it. He couldn't think straight for a few minutes. As if things weren't bad enough.

'What on earth? Now my bank account is being threatened.'

Strange words that I didn't understand, yet I never probed further.

Even after reading the letter for the third time, he was none the wiser. He reconstructed his memories. Speaking out loud now and again, I could piece together what was going on. Our previous flat in Glasgow, the man's name, his young wife, the sketchy details about their reason for moving, the agreement, the removal men, the handing over of title deeds, all that made sense; he remembered it well. But £2,000 was a different story.

'They've got me mixed up with someone else!' He almost choked.

The only thing that had been strange at the time was the couple's reluctance to leave a forwarding address and the duffle bag with old clothes.

'Remember that duffle bag with the old clothes? Can you remember, Alice? Did that go in the bin?'

'Goodness, now you're asking. I don't know. I think Iona used it, but I'm not sure.'

For a second or two, he squeezed his eyes shut and tried to get things into perspective. It was clear he had never seen the £2,000 mentioned in the letter. He wouldn't have forgotten that. He'd get right back to them and tell them they'd made a mistake. But he'd have to admit we kept the bag, although it wasn't clear if it had anything to do with Mrs Smith.

'Maybe your mammy knows something.' He pressed his lips together and looked at the floor.

At eight o'clock the next night, Mammy and Iona returned from their holiday. They had barely stepped through the door when Da jumped up and offered to help with their luggage. He suggested Iona get herself off to her bedroom as soon as possible where I was waiting for her. Iona agreed after pouring a glass of orange juice and sneaking two chocolate digestive biscuits. He saw what she'd done, but tonight it didn't matter. After they exchanged some pleasantries, he practically threw Mammy the letter from Hastings.

'Read it!' he instructed.

She did and felt her heart pumping the hardest it had for years.

'Do you remember anything about it?' he demanded.

She threw the offending article back at him.

'No... I certainly don't!' she retorted, but then opened her eyes wide as she looked at him. She'd just used her posh voice and gave a little snort. Trying to compose herself, she bit into her bottom lip and couldn't wait to tell me later.

'I don't think this is funny in the least,' he continued. 'I have to get in touch with them. They think I've got £2,000 of this Mr Smith's money. If I remember right, the only thing that was unusual after these folks left was the duffle bag. Whatever happened to that?'

'Iona took it to school ages ago with her gym kit and never brought it back. She lost the lot. You know what she's like. There's no way anyone's going to want an old duffle bag back. Why is it so important?' she ventured, having dispensed with her posh voice.

'It's probably not important; I'm just speaking my thoughts. I certainly didn't get any money from them. Did you?'

'How on earth would I get money from them? And £2,000, are you joking?' She avoided revealing anything about her windfall.

'Well, it might have been given to someone else and Mrs Smith is confused.' His tone was a combination of concern and confusion.

Da worried about how it would all end. A while later, he said he had spent a few sleepless nights wondering if he would somehow need to pay £2,000 or if Shug Munro would appear at the door.

Over the next few weeks, the odd phone call from a public phone box ensured the £2,000 situation died a death. Da had convinced the company in Bournemouth that Mrs Smith was completely mistaken; he knew nothing of the money, although he mentioned the bag containing items of clothing. Once the legal representative had mentioned this to Mrs Smith, it triggered her memory. It hadn't been the Edens who had promised to invest the money; it had been her husband's friend who liked to dress as a woman. A second letter arrived for Da, which acknowledged his side of events.

He also found a solution to the Sheena situation. Without her knowledge, he asked his boss for a shift and route change, and two weeks later, he was able to breathe a sigh of relief. Their paths never crossed again and the following month he heard that Sheena and her husband had moved out of town to open a newsagent's shop in

Oban. Da disposed of all the letters and felt he could move on with his life.

Mammy, meanwhile, admitted to me she was happy knowing that she had managed to live the high life for a while without Da being conscious of it. She smiled and clapped her hands, knowing that she had one up on him. Wondering if she missed something when she found the £200, she mentally kicked herself for not double-checking the clothes again. There was every possibility she had overlooked another tidy sum, but she contented herself knowing that she'd been able to experience another side of life with what she had found. Even though she didn't have any cash left, Mammy still had her special purchases.

Chapter 9

Da had taught us we should never borrow nor lend and not to leave money lying around because it could tempt other people to steal. Of course, out in the wicked world that was likely to happen, but I felt things should be safe in our Christian household. Still, Da left nothing anywhere. Items from his pockets were never on display and seldom was he seen handling money.

    Once I was of age to work after school, I secured a part-time job on Friday evenings and all day Saturday packing customers' bags in a local supermarket. One Friday, I was rubbing my hands with glee; I'd had my first tip from a delighted lady; she'd given me 6d which, once home, I proudly showed to Mammy and laid it on the display cabinet. For the next couple of hours, I went about doing whatever I had to do upstairs before coming down for supper. I didn't see Da that evening because he was on a late shift and the next day he was on an extra early shift. When I went downstairs the following morning, I went to get my 6d. It wasn't there. As Mammy made breakfast in the kitchen, I asked her about it. She didn't know but suggested someone might have pushed it under the doily on top of the cabinet.

I looked again. 'No, it's not there. My money's gone.' I flung my jacket on and headed off to my part-time job.

When I arrived home later that day, I found Da sitting in his chair, ready to open the newspaper.

I told him my problem, not accusatory, but with a concerned voice. I pointed at the cabinet.

'I put a 6d up there yesterday and now it's gone. I've asked Mammy, and she hasn't seen it.'

He craned his neck slightly. 'Oh, I took it. I thought it was mine.'

I asked him where it was now and if I could have it back, but he told me he had put it towards buying his daily newspaper. I struggled to understand what he had done. Knowing that he left nothing lying around, he had taken something, money of all things, without even asking if it belonged to anyone else. I couldn't hide my disbelief and sheer disappointment and walked out of the room. I never got my 6d back and never forgot that this Christian man didn't practice what he preached. He wasn't an honest man in my eyes. He couldn't resist storing up money, even if it meant stealing.

However, I wasn't quick to think this was all Da's doing. Strangely enough, Mammy remained silent during our discussion. On reflection, there could be another side to this. If Mammy had said she had no idea who the 6d belonged to, I wouldn't have put it past her to point it out to Da, asking if it was his. He would have jumped at the opportunity to have it if Mammy said it wasn't hers. Another chance to put a wedge between Da and me.

But he had another way of storing up money, one that caused havoc once discovered.

The summer holidays finally arrived. With Iona, I lay longer in bed and chatted about our yearly camping trip. The day before we were due to go, Da was at work and Mammy took me aside. An already opened brown envelope appeared from her apron pocket. She told me it had arrived the day before, addressed to Mr Adam Eden. As a teenager, I knew little about privacy, but I questioned whether it was right to be opening someone else's mail. Although taken aback that Mammy had been so bold as to pocket the envelope, it intrigued me. Out of it came a small, flat book, a bank book. She leafed through the pages and pointed out regular deposits, which in total amounted to just over a thousand pounds. The name at the top of the first page was Adam Eden. With nothing to accompany the mysterious bank book, the only clue was a Glasgow postmark.

As we looked at each page, I felt like a spy, a criminal, a sneak, but I saw a boldness in my mammy that made me think this wasn't the first time she'd interfered with mail that didn't belong to her. I asked why she had opened it in the first place.

'I thought it might have been a gardening book we had ordered, about growing plants from seed.'

The only thing that had been growing was the amount of money in Da's secret bank account. Mammy was reeling, and she asked me what she should do.

I was only fourteen years old and didn't know how to deal with adult issues. My simple response was, 'Ask him what it's all about.'

Even before Mammy had answered me, I could tell by her set mouth that she had already decided to confront him. She sealed the envelope again and placed it in front of the clock. I gathered she wouldn't say anything until later, when she had cooled down. To get into gear, Mammy ran various scenarios by me about the order of events; she would say this and he would say that. Then she would counteract with this and he would react like that. Her control didn't last and, when the confrontation took place, her timing, as usual, was far from impeccable.

Da recalled the incident years afterwards. He had arrived home from his late shift and grabbed the envelope with an idea of what it was. A glance inside confirmed his suspicion. These were payments from his brothers which related to their late father's estate and other repayments of loans he had made to Sam. While we were tucked up in bed and dreaming of our upcoming holiday, he secreted it away in a box, one of his hiding places.

Ever since he had been a boy, Da had created secret places all over the house. Now that he was a married man with a family home, that pursuit was more difficult. He had letters, money and paperwork to hide; he didn't want anyone knowing his business, so he sometimes moved things from beneath the mattress to under the corner of a carpet. Even though he had his own drawer, he didn't think it was a safe place. He was sure Mammy sneaked a look inside, so he often placed a hair or a coin on the edge of the drawer runner to check if anyone had opened it when he wasn't there. He didn't believe Mammy when she said the coin must have fallen when she moved the chest of drawers to use the Hoover. He felt she had discovered most of his nooks and crannies, so he prided himself on moving things from one place to another every week. The loft was his favourite place because he was the only one to venture up there.

On the morning of the holiday, we were up early talking about last-minute things to take with us. Then we would be off to the west coast: hopefully a glorious week of Scottish weather, but it wouldn't matter if it turned out to be miserable. With a new waterproof flysheet for the tent to foil the rain that year, we were almost set. Da packed the larger items in the car first, then came back in for the smaller things, commenting on his meticulous planning and how many Bibles we should take. Mammy was unusually quiet, but I could practically see her mind whirling. She couldn't contain herself any longer. The situation with the bank book had to be addressed.

As Da lifted the last rucksack from the floor, Mammy pointed to the space in front of the clock where she had left the letter. 'So, who was the letter from?'

Without hesitation, he replied, 'A lawyer.'

That wasn't the answer she was hoping for.

'A lawyer?' she scoffed, trying to construct a question. 'Don't you mean a liar?'

He didn't answer.

I stood rooted to the spot. In that split second, I could tell by his stunned expression he knew Mammy had opened the envelope; but he didn't flinch. I wondered if I would have to duck and dive to avoid the flying ornaments which had survived the last battle. There was a long silence. Da wasn't going to talk about the letter and Mammy wasn't getting the chance to say another word; he went outside with the rucksack. I surmised he needed five minutes to figure out a response and silently hope the subject might have been forgotten by the time he came back inside.

He'd better not bank on that, I thought when I saw Mammy's foot tapping.

After he had gone outside, I was astounded to see her dive towards the back door and turn the key to lock him out.

Our front door was always locked, so, as far as Mammy was concerned, he had no way of getting back in. But Da wasn't stupid. The neighbours must have wondered what was going on when they saw him hoist the living room window open, then wiggle his backside in the air as he elbowed his way into the house. Like a cat burglar, he climbed onto the dining room table by the window and, once again, I tensed my stomach in fear of what might happen next.

Iona appeared from upstairs, asking what all the fuss was about; no one answered her. At nine years of age, all she could think about was if we were still going camping. I wasn't sure but I knew, no matter where we were, the next two or three days would be spent in agonising silence while Mammy rid her soul of the anger and frustration over the bank book. If we weren't going camping, our summer would be ruined.

Without another word or a glance at anyone, Da eased himself down from the table, went straight through to unlock the back door and pocket the key. He pranced in and out several times while the camping gear and paraphernalia from the car got unceremoniously dumped around the kitchen and living room floors.

He leapt up the stairs two at a time to the bedroom while the three of us waited with bated breath. Eventually, the strange noises from above stopped, and he returned with a cardboard box and a black suitcase, neither of which we'd ever clapped eyes on. Marching straight out the back door without producing the key, my da put the box and the suitcase in the car's boot and drove off.

Iona and I surveyed the piles of strewn camping gear and rucksacks. Bit by bit, we helped to clear a path to the pantry and, as the hours passed, it finally dawned on us that Da wasn't coming back that afternoon. Even if he returned, there wouldn't have been time to drive to the west coast and pitch the tent. When evening came, we realised we had a big problem. Here we were, three females who would soon have to sleep in a house with an unlocked back door. Before Iona could appreciate the seriousness of the situation, she took a book to bed and settled down for the night. I was the one who had to listen to what might happen to us if some intruder passed by number twenty-two. When I eventually slept, I had a fitful night. My girlish dreams turned into nightmares with visions of animals raiding our pantry for food while the tent was being erected in the living room.

We skirted around the camping gear for a couple of days until we said adios to the holiday, as well as to our da.

None of us did anything special over the next few days. A certain amount of disbelief permeated the atmosphere and Mammy wondered if she should have kept quiet about the bank book and her need to find out where the money came from. Iona went out to play with friends as if it didn't matter where Da was; she was too young to understand the implications of being deserted. I was at a loss; now and again, I caught Mammy staring out of the living room window at nothing.

A few evenings later, when Iona was in bed, I made the mistake of sitting opposite Mammy on one chair from our matching three-piece suite. It was plain grey with red cushions and little wooden legs, the seats not all that comfortable. The mistake wasn't so much the chair but more that I picked the wrong time to join Mammy, who desperately needed someone to talk to. She told me she felt divided in her loyalties. She'd had a couple of days and nights to ponder over the early years of her relationship with Da.

'Do you miss your da?' she asked me.

'Yes and no. I miss him, but I don't miss all the arguing and fighting,' I answered as honestly as I could. 'I feel OK with things the way they are. Do you miss him?'

'I don't know. He does so many things that annoy me, it's not my fault. He's so serious, no fun at all, can't laugh at anything and never wants to spend any money.' Mammy let out an extended sigh and continued. 'When I think about it, he's nearly always been like that. The way he acts, getting angry and things, I could understand it if he was a drinker, but that's not the reason. And some people might say it's all because of what he saw in the war. But lots of men saw terrible things and I'm sure they don't go on like him.'

'So, you must have known what he was like after you'd known each other for a while. Were you ever happy with him?'

She had some unhappy memories which prompted a stream of them: him not turning up for their dates or taking a chocolate before he handed the packet to her. Mammy's mouth twisted in between stories and I imagined her visualising the scenes of each episode, reliving her feelings of disappointment in the man she had once cared for.

She frowned as she continued with stories of times when he spoiled things by being overly strict. She told of occasions when he refused to accept invitations from people who were not part of the church scene. Even if they joined folk who were of the same faith, he found it difficult to converse with them if they weren't speaking about the Bible or some theological issues; it spoiled the visit for the others who weren't as interested. After he stopped taking Mammy to see his family, she accused him of being secretive. She knew she had had nothing good to say about them in the past and had often thrown up their names during arguments, but she felt he could have shared some of their news. She alluded to her eventual unhappiness and frustration with Da when she found he wasn't caring or gentle when they were alone; she didn't elaborate on that to me.

Mammy returned to the present and the unlocked back door. The idea of someone coming in to ravish us, coupled with the more everyday question of what she would do to secure the house when she needed to go out shopping, were genuine concerns. If someone dared to come in to steal personal things, furniture or ornaments that had survived family battles, she wouldn't be able to replace them. I thought I would have been delighted to help a burglar out with the red and grey chairs, meaning I wouldn't have had to sit and listen to Mammy.

The mention of going out shopping, however, brought on another problem. Mammy had no money. Da had it all, including the money he had been squirrelling away each month. My eyes were closing after two hours of listening.

Mammy knew Da was gone from the house, but she wondered if he was gone from the town. She waited a few more days and, as she did, she questioned whether it might be worthwhile going to the bus garage where Da worked, but that might embarrass her. She was indignant and reminded me he was the one who had left. If he didn't want to be with us, she wasn't intending to look for him.

But Mammy was secretly hoping he would walk through the door, even if it was just to leave the housekeeping or return the back door key. That never happened. She reckoned he had no feelings; he was leaving his children to practically starve during the day while waiting to be attacked in their beds at night.

Unlike weekdays, on Saturdays there was only one post delivered around ten-thirty. The first Saturday after Da had left, a letter for Mrs C Eden arrived. It was postmarked Glasgow and I was shown the contents: three postal orders but no note. Mammy had seen postal orders before and had an idea of how they worked. They were like personal cheques, but could only be cashed at a post office. Written in the space beside 'Payee' on one postal order was 'Christina Eden (only)'; on the other two, 'Alice Eden (only)' and 'Iona Eden (only)'. Mammy's postal order was for a larger amount than the other two. It seemed that Da had worked out exactly how much we each needed to live on for a week. It didn't look much to me given that Da was a rich man according to his bank book. Iona was adamant that the postal order with her name was her pocket money. Mammy didn't think so.

Unfortunately, the post office was a distance away and closed at noon on a Saturday. Panic set in as Mammy looked at the time; it was nearly eleven o'clock. She threw on her coat, picked up her shopping bag and, walking swiftly, made her way into town while I waited patiently. Iona drooled over thoughts of what might come after the postal orders had been cashed: rolls, orange juice and maybe ten bars of chocolate.

Nearly an hour later, we saw Mammy turn the corner, rather nimbly in my opinion. As she got closer, my heart sank further into my empty stomach; the bags didn't look heavy and Mammy didn't look happy. We heard the news that the post office wouldn't cash the postal orders because the word *only* meant Da had defaced them. She was told to come back on Monday when the supervisor would be around. Over the weekend, Mammy rummaged in the pantry for make-do meals until they could sort things out at the post office. I was sure of one thing: Da would be somewhere saying grace before tucking into a scrumptious meal.

We skipped the mission on Sunday; the congregation thought we were on holiday anyway and Mammy didn't want to draw attention to Da's absence. We agreed we would go the following week as Mammy hoped Da would be back by then and she wouldn't have any explaining to do.

On Monday, the problem of the postal orders was resolved and from then on they continued to arrive each Saturday, except for the odd occasion when they didn't appear until Monday. That was a difficult time for Mammy. She didn't know whether Da had deliberately not posted the letter on time or if the post had been delayed.

One Friday, Iona looked pleadingly at Mammy as the ice-cream van played its merry tune outside. She asked for a cone, which cost 3d. Mammy produced all she had left, 9d. She took a risk and bought three cones. If the postal orders didn't come the following day, there wouldn't be enough bread for the weekend. Thankfully, the envelope arrived the next morning. Although many people would agree that Da was supporting his family, the uncertainty of the situation created immense stress for Mammy. Her health suffered. She hid a lot from Iona but confided in me. She knew she had to see a doctor to deal with the constant discomfort in her stomach.

We went back to the services at the mission. The congregation were surprised to hear that our camping trip had been postponed; Mammy was vague about her reasons and made some comment about inclement weather in the Highlands. When Da missed all the services, people asked after him. Initially, Mammy didn't want to embarrass herself by saying one thing, then finding out Da had been in touch with someone else and given a completely different reason for his absence. One principle our family held close was to always tell the truth, or rather, not to lie. It seemed acceptable to give a half-truth but never to lie outright; Mammy and Da were masters at that.

She ran through different scenarios. Da might have told a church elder he'd gone to visit his family in Glasgow or had changed his job, both of which were more than likely true. She didn't know which story she should give. To tell the truth would have meant revealing she had found a bank book which upset her and that he had left her and her two girls in an unlocked house. And she didn't know when, or if, he would return.

It became clear four weeks later that Da hadn't been in contact with the mission when the pastor, Mr Ellis, appeared at our door one afternoon. After a heart-to-heart conversation, Mammy finally had to admit Da had mysteriously left home. Mr Ellis was full of concern and assured her that the twenty or so members of the mission would be there for us. If there was anything she needed, she only had to ask, and he encouraged her to continue having fellowship with the female members. Nobody would think any worse of her because she was now a woman on her own with two growing girls. Mammy wasn't so sure. She felt she would be the talk of the town.

True to his word, the pastor arranged for members of the congregation to monitor us. People often invited us out to their homes for Sunday dinner after the morning service and told us to knock on members' doors any time of the day or night. Initially, that sounded very caring and the three of us enjoyed being pampered and attended to. Boxes of goodies would appear. Now and again, someone slipped an envelope of money into Mammy's pocket. Through time, though, she became frustrated if a church member appeared at the door when she was in the middle of tidying up or preparing supper. She felt she could do nothing less than invite them in, offering the customary cuppy.

One gentleman elder of the church, Mr Hyde, made a point of coming to see Mammy more than the others. There was no sinister motive behind his visits; it was only that as a newly retired schoolteacher; he had time on his hands. Mr and Mrs Hyde had recently moved to the area and were keen to integrate themselves by showing love and concern for a fatherless family. But Mammy was tired of Mr Hyde's visits. They ran out of conversation and she felt she could have been doing more worthwhile things, like cleaning out a cupboard, mowing the lawn or converting the loft into living space. Mammy tried to make light of the situation and, given that practically all adults were taller than her, she found it amusing that she had to look down at Mr Hyde. It was hard for her to keep a straight face when she saw him walking up the garden path.

One Saturday afternoon, Mammy spied him just before he got as far as the garden gate and jumped back from the window.

'Alice, Alice!' came the loud whisper. 'Here's Mr Hyde. I don't want to see him. Look, you answer the door and tell him I'm not in.'

I glared at her. We both knew this was an unacceptable lie. My quick-thinking Mammy darted through the living room door and, with one foot on the bottom step, turned to me and grinned.

'Tell him I'm in the bath.' She started up the stairs, then half laughed.

The rattle of the letterbox announced I was now in charge.

'Hello, Alice.' Mr Hyde gazed upwards. 'I've come to see your mum.'

'Oh hi, Mr Hyde. My mammy's in the bath right now.'

Mr Hyde's face showed disappointment, but he composed himself and asked how the family was.

'Everything is fine, thanks. We're all well.' I gave the short but sweet answer, and soon he was on his way.

Once the front door closed, I went upstairs to the bathroom, saw the door was slightly ajar and peered in to see Mammy fully clothed but standing in an empty bath holding a bar of soap. As she stepped out and into her slippers, we burst out laughing. Her story about being in the bath wasn't a half-truth, it was a complete truth.

Chapter 10

Harold and June had known Mammy and Da in the city. They were church goers rather than mission goers, so, because Da wasn't entirely taken with Harold's beliefs, the women spent more time together than the men. June visited Mammy one day in the new town and was amazed at our semi-detached house; she loved the garden and the peaceful surroundings. They both agreed it wouldn't do any harm for Harold to complete an application form for the overspill scheme and see how things worked out. The houses were being snapped up, so Harold was delighted to receive word that a terraced house with back and front gardens was available.

They had to give notice on their flat in the city but couldn't organise a removal van until the following month. Their son, seventeen-year-old Alan, was around two years older than me and had the offer of a storeman's job in the new town to start immediately. With Da out of the picture for almost four months, June asked Mammy if there was any way Alan could stay with us until they all moved through; she agreed. Alan moved in and we reorganised the sleeping arrangements so that he had a room to himself. It was only to be for a few weeks, so nobody was put out for long and Mammy would receive a few pounds for his keep.

When Da had first left, the camping gear had sat for a few days until Mammy asked me to help her move it. We put the tent in the cellar, but the ground sheets, camping stoves and sleeping bags were temporarily put in the living room cupboard where Da used to hang his work coat. Knowing Alan was coming, Mammy decided it was time to move the camping gear. It was taking up too much space. The loft was the best place for it, but she knew the perils of trying to get up there. Alan said he would help to lift things at the weekend, but Mammy wanted to check out how much space was available up there before they started.

It needed a nimble person who could balance on the beams. Young as she was, Iona was game, so Mammy sent her up to survey the scene and report back. After gripping the unsteady ladders, Iona heaved herself inside and Mammy handed her a torch.

'Hold on to the wooden beams, Iona!' Mammy instructed.

As she edged her way along the joists in the semi-darkness, her hand rested on something cold and metal on top of one of the roof beams. Iona picked it up, steadying herself with her other hand. It was the back door key.

We figured it out. Before he had left, Da had hidden the key up there, never thinking for one minute that we would find it. Mammy knew if anyone had ever questioned him about it, he would have been able to say in all honesty that he didn't have the key; it was still in the house. Not a lie, but not a wholly truthful answer. Mammy smiled as she bounced the key in her hand. Now they could lock the back door and stay safe.

'Not so clever now, are you, Adam?' She looked skyward.

One afternoon, I arrived home from school a couple of hours before Alan came in. Mammy was sitting in the living room and told me about a strange event that had taken place earlier in the day. That morning, after we had left for school, Alan had come downstairs while Mammy was standing at the cooker. As she turned to face him, the elastic in her knickers snapped and they landed at her feet. Alan had thrown his hands up in horror and scarpered back up the stairs. Mammy thought it was funny. I wasn't so sure what all this meant, but I was fleetingly concerned about my mammy's state of mind. Alan had picked up his jacket and things for work and ran out of the house with no breakfast. After that, he made a point of never being in the same room alone with Mammy and contacted his mother to tell her to speed things up at her end. Traumatised, he moved out to stay with a workmate. His quick exodus from us persuaded me that there was more to this story, but I never found out.

Maybe it was the absence of a strict father figure for six months or an urge to rebel against the teachings of the Bible, but us girls showed increased signs of restlessness. I was fifteen and mixing with other teenagers, some of whom were older than me and had left school. How grown-up I felt to go out of an evening and meet at the shopping centre or anywhere teenagers could gather. Our group didn't deliberately cause bother, but the people who lived around our meeting place weren't pleased with youths shouting and laughing right outside their living room windows.

The time came when someone had a few cans of beer and cigarettes. No one had money to spare and so it was only the young working men who could afford such luxuries. Some offered cigarettes around the group on the condition that we would share one between two, coupled with a promise to repay the following day. I didn't enjoy smoking but once the others saw I had tried it, although I coughed and spluttered my way through less than half of it, the group branded me as one of them; smoking wasn't a pursuit I continued.

Some kids went to the same secondary school as me and, when we discovered it was relatively easy to dodge classes, two or three of us would stay in the girls' toilets once the bell rang for class. We had to pass the time doing nothing but sitting on a closed toilet pan, whispering for fear of being heard by any teacher who might pass by. It was a boring fifty minutes and not worth it.

When I teamed up with Jenny, who lived on the outskirts of town, life became more exciting. We were in the same class, but Jenny was more mature than me. She took the bus to school, plus she had an older boyfriend who was working and kept her supplied with cigarettes. We decided it would be much better to dodge classes for more than one lesson, perhaps the afternoon or the whole day, and so it started.

We hung around the park in the mornings trying to avoid being seen by truant officers or anyone in authority. Jenny's mother, who was disabled, wasn't overly concerned about us arriving home for lunch then hanging around for the rest of the day; she thought this was all legitimate, and that Jenny had permission to come home and help with household chores. After washing and drying a few dishes, we retreated to Jenny's bedroom to play music and gossip about teenage life. Neither Jenny's parents nor Mammy knew we weren't going to school at all. With Da out of the picture, I felt more daring. If I kept my lunch money, I could take a bus back from Jenny's in time to join the others coming out of school. It didn't occur to us what would happen once we were missed.

After a week of absence, a truancy officer from the school arrived at our house, enquiring about my welfare. Mammy was completely blindsided. When I came home acting as if it had been a normal day, Mammy was waiting. She was livid; feeling a complete idiot not to have grasped what was going on. She screamed and shouted, accusing me of bringing unnecessary problems into the home on top of Da's absence. The moment I mentioned Jenny's name, Mammy flew into another rage.

I escaped upstairs, but she followed. It was only when I felt the sting on my face I realised Mammy had slapped me. She didn't stop. Leathering into me, she got all her frustration out. She never thought to ask what was wrong at school or why I had stayed off, but she asked where I went. The mention of Jenny's house was a further trigger for another round of punching and slapping. She only stopped when I fell off the bed and wet myself. I spent the next month catching up with missed classwork and never played truant again.

Jenny's mother had been upset, but not to the same extent as my mammy. Jenny remained an enormous influence in my life, despite a warning that we shouldn't hang out together. It was only when she told me she thought she might be pregnant and asked me to run away with her if need be that things changed. I agreed, but underneath, I knew it was all too bizarre for me. It wasn't worth another round with my Mike Tyson mother. I was careful not to step out of line; in fact, Mammy didn't have any bother with me in that respect again.

Sadly, Mammy was feeling the strain of having to deal with everyday life without a husband. In the 1960s, there was still criticism and gossip attached to single-parent families even if one partner had died. But it was more than that. She had to make all the decisions and deal with problems like my truancy and the usual scrapes youngsters get into. There was no respite and no one to support her. She had been annoyed at me and reminded me that nine-year-old Iona wasn't a problem child. However, unbeknown to Mammy, Iona was developing her own bad habits.

Madge, Mammy's friend from the city, and her husband Bert, had been given a four-bedroomed council house in the new town, complete with a good sized garden. Although neither of them was religious, Da had shown compassion towards them before he left, realising they wanted a fresh start away from the city. Bert wouldn't have qualified for an overspill house without a job, so Da got him an application form for the bus company. Bert had already driven trucks and was delighted to be offered a position on condition that he spent a week as a trainee driver.

We didn't take to Madge's two rowdy boys, but their little sister, Beth, a gentle child, was almost Iona's age and we liked her. Iona and Beth played in the bedroom, talking about animals and girly things, and Beth showed Iona some trinkets. She didn't like the silver necklace with a panda anymore because her brothers called her Andy

Pandy when she wore it, so Beth donated it to a smiling Iona. In the months that followed, Iona picked up another necklace and two bracelets from other sources. They were 'borrowed' from unsuspecting friends. She showed them to me, but something didn't ring true about their origin. After the pencil and pencil case episode years before, Iona's tastes had changed.

Time went by and Da had been gone for over a year when Iona celebrated her tenth birthday in November. With limited funds, it was impossible for her to get the puppy she had hinted at, so she forced a smile at the drawing paper and the little dog on a chain necklace. Mammy explained things might change before Christmas, which made Iona think maybe Da would send extra money or even return and agree to the sought-after puppy. She couldn't wait.

In the meantime, one day, Iona and I were talking about being afraid. We started off with the usual banter.

'Are you frightened of spiders?'

'No, but I don't like snakes!'

Just stupid girl talk.

Eventually, she blurted out a story that made me sit back.

One afternoon and with three friends, she had stopped off at a house belonging to one of their aunts. Aunt May had welcomed the girls, and they played with her toddler for half an hour before Iona asked if she could go to the toilet. They directed her to the top of the stairs. All the upstairs doors were closed and by accident, Iona opened a bedroom door. She looked around. On a dressing table, she saw a dish with what looked like rings and next to it lay a purse.

Iona glanced behind, saw the coast was clear, and took a swift step towards the dressing table. In a matter of seconds, a small silver band and two ten-shilling notes from the purse were in her pocket. She left the room and found the toilet. When it was time for them to leave, each of the girls paid a visit upstairs, then they set off. Iona said she had to go straight home where she secreted her stash under some socks in her drawer. The ring fitted her middle finger, but she was careful not to wear it to school, only on a Sunday to the mission where her school friends would never see it. Iona was sure Mammy believed she had borrowed it from a friend. And every morning on her way to school, Iona stopped at the local newsagents and enjoyed a plentiful supply of ready salted crisps and Mars bars.

It was two weeks later when the oldest of her friends said Aunt May wondered who had gone into her bedroom the day of their visit. Iona asked why.

'She can't find a silver ring her grandmother gave her and she said money was missing from her purse.'

'Why are you asking me about it? More folk than me were in the house!' Iona had turned away.

She put spending on hold, and the ring was in a bin the next day. The only thing Iona worried about was anyone coming to the door to ask Mammy about the missing jewellery. That never happened. Iona breathed a sigh of relief and decided that being dishonest wasn't worth it. She must have been worried because she made a vow to herself in front of me. That was the end; she had enough things of her own. Iona even tried to figure out what had driven her to take things that didn't belong to her and, although she couldn't understand it, she implied she was trying to distract herself from the unhappiness she felt at home. It seemed like everybody in the world, except for Iona and me, had two happy parents to spend birthdays and Christmases with.

As it was, we got an extra pound or two on our weekly postal orders from Da at these special times, but Mammy encouraged us to buy essentials instead of what she said were unnecessary treats.

Granny still lived alone in the city. It wasn't unusual for months to pass in between her visits or contact of some description. Being a spontaneous woman, instead of writing a letter to inform us she would like to pay a visit, she often turned up at the door having taken an hours' bus journey then hitching a lift in a lorry for the last three miles from the bus station. One day, I came home to discover Granny had been and gone, bringing news of Da.

They had met at a church service where he asked her to pass a message on to Mammy. A year and a half had passed since he had left, and he hoped there would be an opportunity for reconciliation. His life had become stagnant and, if there was no chance of him and Mammy patching things up, he was intending to leave Scotland for good and go to live in Germany. He would wait for a month for Mammy's response.

Even though we loved Da, Iona and I had been happy without the conflict his presence brought. Iona enjoyed having a mother's love to herself and I thought having him back wasn't a good idea, but the situation tore at Mammy.

'It's all right for you, you and Iona have each other. I have no one,' she admitted to me. 'We could meet him for a day and see what comes of it.'

Two weeks later, we took the bus to the city to meet him. Da immediately spotted Mammy and a smiling Iona;

she had changed little. I came over bashfully; I was a gangly sixteen-year-old, and he hardly recognised me. After a brief exchange, we made our way to a nearby café where we caught up on news and then, after Da paid the bill, we set off to his flat nearby.

It was a typical ex-army man's flat; minimalistic and tidy. To my horror, but to Iona's delight, he had a yellow bird, Ricky, in a cage. Da gave us a few pennies and sent us off to buy some sweets while they talked about the intricacies of their relationship. By the time we returned, they had decided. Da was coming back, complete with the budgie and the promise of a television.

Mammy busied herself preparing for Da's return. Clearing out old clothes and cleaning every corner of the house made her feel like a wife again. After dispensing with most of his furniture, Da returned home two weeks later with a newer model of the Mini he left with. He successfully applied for his old job driving buses and reappeared at the mission. Mammy was happy now she didn't have the worry of postal orders and could afford to present bigger portions of tastier meals to us plus, having spent over a year on his own, Da appreciated what was involved in running a house. He suggested that Iona and I take a turn to do more and give Mammy a hand about the house. That suggestion was met with long faces and reluctance from us until he used the television as a weapon. No helping equalled no programmes.

My parents continued the housekeeping arrangement, which had started all those years ago after Mammy had complained about Jessie's wage in the dairy. Money was seldom mentioned and each Friday, Da left Mammy her housekeeping next to the crinoline lady on top of the display cabinet. Eventually, this throwback to the time before he left rekindled some of the animosity between them.

If the housekeeping wasn't there on a Friday night, Mammy was tense; the arrangement did not involve her asking. She didn't want to give him the satisfaction of what she termed begging for it. Knowing full well that if she had been given the money in the afternoon, she could have popped out to the shops, Da could sometimes sit all evening reading while she had to rummage in the pantry and try to make an evening meal from practically nothing. She was sure he was deliberately making her wait. Maybe the money would be left for her after the shops had closed on a Friday, maybe not until the Saturday morning or even a Saturday afternoon as he left for his back shift. Then she had to rush to the local Co-op and pick up what she could before the fresh fruit and vegetables were gone. If Da wasn't around to take her shopping in the car, she had to catch the bus or walk. She would set off fuming, knowing she had to carry home whatever was left on the Co-op shelves in her oversized shopping bags. He never helped because that was a woman's job. If Da decided not to part with the housekeeping in time, it messed the entire weekend up.

He was barely back six months when things turned sour between them. The disagreements and bad feelings returned and permeated everything; as I walked home after school, my stomach tightened in fear of what I might face. Iona clung to Mammy and practically ignored Da. The tension was stressful for everyone, but especially for Mammy, who was experiencing growing discomfort in her stomach despite her prescribed medication. Something was wrong again, and she promised herself she would see a doctor.

Unlike me, Iona was an animal lover and adored Ricky. She gravitated to dogs and cats or any other animal that crossed her path. Horse riding was her favourite, but regular lessons were too expensive, so she mucked out the stables for a few hours on horseback. Convinced that riding was getting rid of Iona's puppy fat, Mammy encouraged her and agreed to lessons now and again if Iona did chores around the house. Da gave us a few coins if we wrote out some verses from the Bible, and once Iona discovered she needed extra money for horse riding, she couldn't wait for him to come home and offer to write out a verse or two. Sometimes that worked, but sometimes he laughed at her childish request; he could see right through her.

Iona also befriended people who needed a volunteer dog walker. It was almost enough to satisfy her desire for a pet. The rule from Mammy was – no dogs allowed in the house. There was enough work to be done without cleaning up dog hairs. In the main, Iona observed the rule but when she was sure Mammy would be out, she arrived home with one of the three dogs she walked. If, by any chance, anyone was home, the excuse was that she needed to go to the toilet and couldn't wait. Mammy was a bit of a sniffer dog herself because she could tell when Iona broke the rule.

One day, we played a trick on Mammy. One of my friends had been to a joke shop and was the proud owner of an oversized dog poo. After borrowing it for the night, I showed it to Iona. She laid it on the bathroom floor and we waited, doubled up quietly, as Mammy climbed the stairs.

'Iona. Iona. Have you had a dog in here?'

It took Mammy a few minutes to realise what we'd done. She joined in the laughter and for the first time in ages; we saw our mammy could still appreciate the funny side of life.

When Ricky became ill and died around the same time as the dog walking was becoming a chore, Iona pleaded for a rabbit. Mammy wasn't quick enough to refuse, so Iona jumped in and reminded her that the animal wouldn't be in the house.

'Ask your da,' was the reply.

Da welcomed the idea of the rabbit. Providing Iona would look after it, he would build a hutch. It was a done deal, and Snowy appeared a couple of weeks later. Within a few months, though, it all bored Iona because she had to do the work on her own and she was limited to where she could go with a rabbit. What she really wanted was a puppy; she kept reminding everyone. It didn't take too long to convince Mammy and Da that it was a better option; she could get some exercise by walking it and it wouldn't cost any more than a rabbit, according to Iona.

With the rabbit and hutch deposited at Iona's friend's house three streets away, Max arrived. It surprises me now that neither a ten-year-old nor Mammy and Da had envisaged the work surrounding a puppy. I made it clear from the start; I wasn't having anything to do with it.

Dog walking became less frequent, and Iona left Max in the garden alone. The cost of dog food and other bits and pieces sunk in with Mammy. Da certainly wasn't footing that bill.

Mammy decided enough was enough when Iona got fed up opening the door for Max and, months later, I learned of his fate. Without telling Iona, Mammy made a bus trip to the city with Max.

Spying a red telephone box on a busy city street, she encouraged the puppy to come in along with her. He sniffed around. Then she opened the door to escape while a treat distracted him. The heavy phone box's door closed just as Max turned his head and saw her leave. Mammy averted her eyes; she couldn't look back; she daren't change her mind.

The bus she needed to take out of the city was turning the corner and heading her way. She half ran to join the queue, paid and then scrambled towards a back seat. Her heart was pounding; she couldn't tell anyone what she had done. The bus took off and stopped at the next set of traffic lights a few yards down the road. Pedestrians cut across, and it took Mammy by surprise to see a young man crossing the road and snuggling into Max, who was licking his face with great gusto. He had rescued the puppy. The bus stopped long enough for her to see Max and his new owner become lost in the throng of people. It looked like the young man would have unending compassion for a little abandoned puppy.

After school that day, it took Iona a full five minutes to call on the puppy. My aproned Mammy stood at the sink preparing vegetables.

'Have you seen Max?' Iona eventually asked.

'I was going to ask you the same thing. What happened this morning? Max hasn't been here all day,' Mammy truthfully reported.

'What do you mean?' Iona's eyes widened.

'Did you close the gate after you left?'

Mammy didn't feel bad about being sly. She said no more.

The whole thing gutted Iona. When she could, she went in search of Max over the next few days, even missing her favourite television programmes. It dawned on Mammy that Iona was spending more time looking for Max than she had done caring for him. The only thing Da offered to Iona as he shrugged his shoulders was, 'No animals will ever come to stay again.'

Not long after, Iona came home from school to see bed sheets had become tangled around the clothes lines. She trailed her schoolbag along the garden path as though it were a reluctant puppy until she almost collided with Mammy at the back door. I heard the commotion from my open bedroom window.

'Are you going out?' She stopped to let Mammy pass.

'I'm just going to bring the washing in.'

Iona dumped her bag on the living room floor and threw her blazer over the arm of the couch. Thoughts of food, as usual, prevailed. There was a moment of confusion when she opened the pantry door and glanced inside. A box of fish dressing and some self-raising flour sat on the shelf that normally held pancakes and packets of biscuits. Her eyes scanned the other two shelves. Nothing but jars of pickles and marmalade.

From the upstairs window, I saw Mammy stumble as a gust of wind caught her breath on her way up the two back steps; a sock and my underwear fell from the overflowing wash basket.

'Mammy, where's all the food? There's no bread or anything.'

'Under the table. In the green bag.' Mammy nodded toward two shopping bags partially obscured by the sides of the oversized flowery tablecloth.

Iona lifted the bag and placed it on the table. Rummaging through the fruit, she found a packet of biscuits, a few loose chocolate teacakes, and an almost finished loaf of bread.

'Why are some of these things opened?' She lifted the tablecloth and brought the other bag forward to see a pint of milk, a packet of cold meat, an opened half pound of butter and a small bottle of diluting orange juice. 'Why is our food in bags and not in the cupboard?'

'He's due back in two hours and I'm going out. I'm taking the bags with me so that he won't have anything to eat,' she announced as though it was as common a household chore as folding the washing.

It wasn't difficult for Iona to hold back with her questions because the rumble from her stomach told her the two teacakes were more important than the answer to why Mammy was prepared to walk the streets with the contents of our pantry in her shopping bags.

With chocolate still coating her tongue, Iona didn't need much of an excuse to ignore her history homework – it was the weekend after all – and sidled back into the living room where Mammy was grappling with a double bed sheet.

'Make sure none of that food is sitting on the table.' She raised her voice. 'Is it all away?'

Iona nodded.

'What's happening? Is Da not getting any tea tonight?'

I arrived downstairs to see Mammy patting the last towel down on the pile of folded washing before running a hand through her hair as if to clear her mind. Her skin was pale next to her unbuttoned brown cardigan. She fanned herself with an old magazine.

'I know this is hard for you to understand, but if he's not going to leave the housekeeping in time for me to get to the shops, I don't see why he should get to eat.'

'But what about me and Alice?'

She said she had been dreaming about the usual Friday night mince and potatoes. The offer of scrambled eggs on toast wasn't even a close second.

Iona rolled her eyes as Mammy brought the toast out of the grill, served the eggs, then left the kitchen. We sat down, eyed the plates and looked towards each other at the same time.

'Da's not getting any food tonight. Mammy's got it all in her bags and she's taking it out for a walk,' Iona whispered cupping her hands around her mouth.

She spluttered at my expression.

Both bags were placed at the back door a few minutes later; nothing was said while Mammy buckled the belt on her raincoat.

'Where are you going?' Iona asked.

'Out. That's all you need to tell him if he asks.'

At that, Mammy picked up the two bags and asked me to close the door behind her.

Iona broke the silence after her chore of washing up was over.

'Alice, are you still going out?'

'Yes, I'm leaving in ten minutes.' I turned before I made my way upstairs and saw Iona on the couch, twisting and turning the button on her school blazer.

What I didn't know then was that her eyes were brimming over. When she heard me battering down the stairs a few minutes later, she leaned over towards her school bag. I was about to fly past her without a second glance, but I stopped when she spoke.

'So, it's my job to deal with him?' Iona blinked away a second wave of tears and glanced at the clock. I sat down beside her. Fifteen minutes until the hour of reckoning.

It took five minutes for Da to greet us, rid himself of his coat and haversack, then wash his hands.

'Where's Mammy?'

'She's out and I don't know where she's gone and there's nothing to eat and that's all I know!' Iona looked out the window, knowing there was no chance of Mammy appearing to explain herself.

As if he needed proof, Da wrenched the pantry door open. I kept quiet.

'Oh!' He stood back without closing the door. 'So, what's happened?'

Fumbling over her words, Iona repeated what she had been told to say without alluding to the real reason for the food supplies being removed from the house.

'And have you eaten?' he asked with a sucking in of his lips.

Satisfied that Mammy had fed us, Da put on his work jacket again and left the house. He had cottoned on to Mammy's game. Ten minutes later, the speckles of raindrops outside turned to lashings of rain streaming down the living room window. Being dry in the house's safety should have been a comfort, but Iona shivered, then sighed. There was tension lurking in the shadows. Another ruined weekend.

The walk-in cupboard off the living room doubled as a place for hanging Da's coat and jackets for his job, so that when he left early or arrived home late, he wasn't disturbing the rest of the family by opening and closing wardrobe doors. The odd jacket belonging to me or Iona ended up in the cupboard, too. One day, Da announced to Mammy he was sure I was smoking.

'What makes you think that?' she asked.

'The cupboard – it smells of cigarettes and it's been like that since last night,' he replied.

Once he had gone to work, Mammy went into the cupboard and, sure enough, there was a distinct smell of stale cigarette smoke. Starting with mine, she drew the coats and jackets towards her and had a good sniff. Yes, there was a smell of smoke on each one. Since it was a relatively pleasant, dry afternoon, Da had only taken his jacket and so she smelled his hanging coat. It was stinking of smoke; much stronger than what was coming from the other jackets. This was the offending article, not mine. She challenged him on his return.

'By the way, you're right about the smell in the cupboard. It's sickening. I smelled every jacket and coat in there and, if I didn't know better, I'd say you were a heavy smoker!' she snorted.

He was speechless. As he felt his anger rising, he only sucked in his lips. He had jumped to a conclusion about me and would never admit he was wrong. It developed into unnecessary mudslinging and an argument that lasted three days until he finally announced that, from then on, he'd hang his coat in the cellar outside.

Once the disagreements flared up again between Mammy and Da, they reached a new level of intimidation. There was still the throwing of ornaments, books and food, but the threats and suggestions from Mammy were more worrying. She told us that knives were missing from the kitchen drawer and implied that Da could be the culprit, so she was intending to buy a hammer because Da was more unpredictable than ever. We were fearful when situations that she could have dealt with agreeably led to fierce animosity.

During some arguments, Mammy scratched and bit Da when she got close enough. He decided the best way to get protection was from the police and, when he sensed he was within a hair's breadth of being attacked, he left the house and called the local police station from the nearest phone box.

The police got to know our house and let it be known that they had more important things to attend to than a domestic incident. They couldn't understand why Da couldn't control his wife. On one visit, Iona was whimpering, and I was crying my eyes out when the police asked me to step into the kitchen. They closed the door behind them and waited for me to calm down.

'What do you think we can do to help?' the taller policeman asked.

'I don't know. I honestly don't know. This has been going on for years. We had peace when my da was away. Now that he's back, nothing's changed.'

The other policeman came up with a solution.

'What would you think if we charged your mum with breach of the peace? She would have to go to court and she'll be told to calm things down or there'll be repercussions.'

'I think we should try anything we can to stop this!'

I looked at my tear-stained face in the mirror of a small corner cabinet. As a sixteen-year-old, it embarrassed me to have swollen, red eyes in front of two men I'd never met before. They nodded and moved back to the living room to speak to Mammy privately.

I seem to remember spending the rest of the day in my bedroom, afraid to go downstairs even after the police left. I imagine Iona and I would have sat for ages upstairs, leafing through teenager's magazines or trying to enjoy a few chapters of a book.

Chapter 11

It hadn't even been a year since Da's return when Mammy felt unwell again. The pain had moved from her stomach to her side and drove her to bed some afternoons. Madge had visited one day and insisted on making a doctor's appointment for Mammy.

When it had finally come through, she told him it felt as though a gigantic piece of chewing gum inside was restricting her movement. Also, she could now feel something solid if she pressed her fingers into her left side.

Mammy received two letters ten days after the police visit. One was from a specialist clinic: her X-ray appointment at the hospital was confirmed for 12th of February. The other informed her she had to appear at court on 10th February. The court date was poignant because it was my parents' wedding anniversary; there was no chance of a celebration. The court charged her £10 (around £200 in today's money) and told her to behave herself. She paid the fine but couldn't control her temper tantrums for long.

She had to wait three weeks for the result of her X-ray. The consultant broke the news to Mammy that there was a growth that shouldn't be there. The only solution was an operation to remove it as it was causing her so much pain and pressing against other organs. She was told it was urgent and given a date to be admitted to hospital; only then would they be able to tell her exactly what was going on in her body.

She didn't say a word to Da about any appointments. She told me when her admission date came through and gave me the job of making sure Iona was up and out to school in the mornings for the few days she would be out of commission. I could visit the hospital, but on no account was I to tell Da. Once again, Mammy was leaving him out and didn't seem to care how it affected me. He was to suffer for involving the police, her court appearance and £10 fine. We girls would have school lunches and Mammy planned with a neighbour to bring some food over to the house for us every second evening; Da was to fend for himself.

On the afternoon of Mammy's admission to hospital and despite the rest of us being at home, Da never asked where she was and he headed up to bed around nine o'clock; he had an early rise in the morning. The following afternoon, I took time off school and made my way by bus to visit Mammy. I dressed as smartly as I could, given the limited wardrobe I had, and carried a dinky little bag which my friend had lent me.

Outside the hospital, the size of the place completely overwhelmed me and I wondered how on earth I would find my way around. One woman told me there was a shortcut through the basement, so I followed the throng of visitors. The pipes that gurgled and spluttered along the ceiling scared me, but the sterile hospital smell didn't hit me until we emerged into a stairwell. Visitors strictly adhered to the visiting times, so I joined the others waiting outside the ward. At two o'clock precisely, a stern-faced matron opened the door, and I hesitantly made my way in, searching for room number eight. I found Mammy asleep in one of four beds. Standing there, bewildered and at a loss, I was in a daze until the woman in the next bed spoke.

'Do you know her?'

'Yes. It's my mammy, but she's not wakened yet.'

'You can come and sit here until she wakes up. My visitors aren't here yet.'

I sat down and chatted briefly to the woman who told me she hoped to get out the following day. She was missing home and her children. At that, her visitors arrived, so I moved my chair to sit inches from Mammy. The chattering of the others in the room hung in the air as I looked closely at the frail-looking person in the bed and the tubes connected to her nose and mouth. It was a frightening experience. I bowed my head as my tears dripped onto my new purple mini-skirt, then felt a hand on my shoulder.

'What are you doing here?' a nurse asked.

Her voice was enough to rouse my mammy, who had opened her eyes in time to see my tear-stained face and the nurse ushering me out by the arm.

'Oh, Alice,' Mammy whispered, as I disappeared through the ward doors.

The nurse led me to a desk where a senior member of staff sifted through files. She brought out Mammy's records and asked how old I was and where Da was.

'I'm sixteen. My da's at work. My mammy doesn't want him to know she's in here,' I answered, sniffling.

'Well, you shouldn't be here. On the day of an operation, there are only certain people allowed in.' Moving her head back and forth, the nurse ran her index finger over a sheet of paper. 'Your da's down here as next of kin. You're far too young to be put in this situation. Get off home and don't worry, we'll deal with this. Come back in a couple of days when she'll be brighter. Your mum will be here for a week at least.'

They left me to find my way out of the hospital and up to the bus station.

I decided that if Da was at home when I got back; I was going to tell him.

He was there, making a cup of tea.

'Oh, Alice, I thought you'd be in your school uniform.' Da looked me up and down, then followed me into the living room.

'Da, listen. I've got something to tell you,' I announced as I put the little bag down and sat on the couch. 'It's Mammy, she's in hospital. She had an appointment to go in yesterday but didn't want to bother you with it all. Today I've been up to see her because she had an operation this morning.'

My wide-eyed da sat back in his chair; he didn't appear to know what to say, so I continued.

'It wasn't a problem for me to go up, but the nurses were annoyed because I was there and not you. And I was crying.' I blurted it out before I could think of a way to soften the blow.

'Well, I... I... I can't think why she didn't tell me. How could I go to the hospital if I didn't even know she was there, never mind having an operation? What kind of operation? What's all this about?' He fumbled over his words.

I told Da that Mammy had been spending longer in bed when he wasn't around, complaining of a pain in her side. Also, she had asked me if I wanted to feel the bit that was annoying her, but I had reeled back in horror. I knew about Mammy's visit to the doctor and the medication that didn't work. I could tell him of her appointment where she had told the specialist about a feeling of something like chewing gum, gripping her insides. There was an X-ray that showed something was growing inside her. That's as much as I had been aware of until I heard about her admission to hospital. This operation was going to reveal what the extent of the problem was.

'Don't you go back up there,' Da insisted. 'Leave it with me. Tell me the ward number and I'll contact them. I'll go up from now on.'

I was sure Mammy would be mad at me for spilling the beans, but this was all too much. Although I risked her wrath, it was worth it because now the burden had been shared and mostly lay at Da's door.

A couple of days later, after he had seen Mammy and spoken to the ward staff, he suggested I go back to visit and take Iona with me. It turned out she wasn't as opposed to Da's visits as she had made out to me. The idea had been to exclude him; it didn't matter for how long and a few days was enough for her to make him feel left in the dark about something so serious.

They discharged her after eight days and she built up some strength to continue with life. Da had a good idea what was ahead health-wise for Mammy, but he only hinted to me, we weren't told anything concrete.

Da had control of everything because he controlled the money. Over the next year, Mammy developed an ever-increasing level of spite to exact her revenge. She liked to see him squirm; she liked to see him confused; she liked to see him put in a corner because of his fanatical, religious beliefs and his never-ending need for order and penny-pinching. He wouldn't have been found lacking very often because Da purported to do everything in the open. However, he had a major failing that stemmed from his frugal nature. If he saw an opportunity to get something for nothing, he couldn't resist. And Mammy knew this.

One of Da's commitments to the mission was to deliver religious tracts, and he had agreed to cover the whole of the town within a year. Normally, he made his deliveries in the evenings because he hoped people would be home by then and he might speak about how to save their souls. After finishing his early shifts at two o'clock, if he had tracts in his pocket, he would deliver to the houses and flats he passed on his way home.

He was unusually late leaving work one wintry Monday after his early shift because his boss had told him to come into the office. He had something to say. The boss asked if Da would be interested in an inspector's post. The suggestion took him by surprise. This would mean a rise in pay and perhaps a bit of recognition for what he considered his thorough manner and meticulous honesty. He said he would think about it and, for one of the few times in his life, he stopped to have a cup of tea in a café. It was the dingiest café around, but it was the cheapest and right up his street. He thought over the job offer and weighed up the pros and cons. As Da walked home, he remembered he had a few tracts, enough to cover about fifteen houses. He took the straight route down Burnbank

Street. It was semi-dark, although it wasn't quite four o'clock. It had snowed a few hours before, but most of it had turned to slush; such was winter life in Scotland.

Earlier that same day, around noon on her way back from the grocer's, Mammy had negotiated the snow-white pavements and spied what initially looked like a wooden spoon partially covered with a smattering of snow. She never knew why, but she kicked it and saw it was a screwdriver. The handle didn't look damaged; in fact, the whole thing looked new, so she picked it up and dropped it inside her shopping bag, laughing to herself as she thought she was getting just like Da, looking for something for nothing.

After trudging the last few yards home, she laid her bags down on the kitchen floor, removed her gloves, and kicked off her sodden boots. Once she dealt with the shopping, she examined the screwdriver with care. She was pretty sure it was a Phillips screwdriver because they designed the tip like a little flower. Da had gone on about how special these were and that they couldn't be used for normal screws. His Phillips had been destroyed many moons ago.

For a fleeting moment, she thought Da might be happy to have it, and then she dismissed the idea. He hadn't bought it or got it as a present, so he might say it was sinful to keep it. If she presented him with it, there would be twenty questions. She would hang onto it because his precious toolbox was forbidden territory now anyway. No one could move it, let alone open it, unless they wanted to start World War III. Previously, Da kept it in the downstairs cupboard, but he discovered it had been disturbed when Iona had gone looking for a hammer one day. He was so annoyed he gave it a new home, the highest possible shelf in the cellar outside. Having a spare screwdriver would solve this problem for Mammy. She could build up her own supply of handy gadgets to either use or threaten Da with.

Any jobs that needed to be done around the house or garden were his domain and he had implied that a woman wasn't capable of doing intricate jobs that required specialist tools. However, my resourceful mammy fancied herself as a practical woman, and she was right. She had learned to dismantle and clean things that weren't working, such as the vacuum cleaner or her sewing machine. Here was a great opportunity to build up her own toolbox. He needn't know about it and she'd be able to broaden her horizons by fixing the loose sideboard door, tightening the toilet seat, or even taking a joinery course.

More snow fell and, the next day, Tuesday, in the local Co-op, rumours flitted between the small group of women, including the local gossip, Sadie. Mammy was excited to tell me the story, even before she took off her snow drenched coat. A man had been found dead in his terraced house three streets away from our house. From what they had discussed, Mammy gathered the victim had lived with another man. In the mid-1970s, that was an unusual and generally unacceptable way of life, and in a small town, it was certainly a topic for discussion.

She didn't normally have the luxury of reading the daily newspapers; that was for the man of the house, although she was allowed to read any part of the paper, provided Da had read it first. A day after gathering her first lot of information at the Co-op, she broached the subject of the murder with him.

'Is there anything in the paper about that man from Burnbank Street?' she casually mentioned.

'Yes, if you can believe what you read. There're a few sentences tucked into the corner. Here.' He passed her the front page of the *East Coast Herald,* still joined to the back page. According to the article, fifty-year-old Joseph Davidson's body had been discovered by his friend, Victor, when he arrived home after work. A contact number was given for anyone who thought they might have seen anything unusual.

Da went to work and Mammy couldn't wait to get back to the Co-op.

The locals were exchanging whatever news was circulating without knowing which parts were genuine and which were not. Sadie had pieced together everything she had heard and told Mammy the latest, which included her own version to make folk think she was in the know.

She said that the dead man had been found sitting in his armchair wearing a zip-up cardigan and casual trousers, with his tartan slippers still on his feet and his glasses lying on the rug in front of the fire. Victor had gone completely crazy when he saw him. Running out into the street, slipping and sliding through the slush, he had cried out in an unholy manner.

'Help, help, help me! It's Joe, it's Joe. Help, help. Somebody call the police!' he had screamed.

Telephones were few and so it took a few minutes to rouse the owners of a party line. They had dialled 999 while some kind people took Victor under their wing. Once the local police arrived, the house was cordoned off. It had been hours before Victor was allowed back inside.

The police had questioned those nearby about what they saw and whether they knew anything about Joe's way of life. Two men living together threw up all kinds of questions. How close were they to the folk in the vicinity? Did anyone show a dislike for the way they lived?

Mammy's eyes widened when Sadie told her a man wearing a dark uniform had been seen walking away from Joe's door that Monday afternoon; he needed to be found to help with police enquiries. But the most alarming part of Sadie's story was that there had been a screwdriver sticking out the top of Joe's head; she described how the matted blood had created dark patches on his slicked-back, greying hair as if she had witnessed the scene for herself.

By Thursday, the story had got as far as the baker's and, as Mammy ordered a plain loaf, she thought what a coincidence that she'd found a screwdriver on the Monday, the same day as the murder had occurred and in the same street. She knew hers wasn't the one that had killed the man and she knew she wasn't in any trouble, but she just didn't like the idea of screwdrivers anymore. As soon as she got home, she took the dreaded article out of the pantry where she had hidden it and put it under some tablecloths in a sideboard drawer, although she wasn't convinced that was any better a hiding place.

By Friday, the snow had cleared and more folk were out and about. Mammy made an apple pie while Da busied himself with the slack hinge on the outside cellar door. Even if she had known how to fix it, the hinge was too high for her. Da's toolbox was lying open on the path when nature called him upstairs. Mammy saw her chance. She rushed to the bottom drawer of the sideboard and lifted an embroidered tablecloth to reveal the first item that was supposed to have been for her new toolbox. I appeared at that moment and she put her forefinger to her lips which told me I was to say nothing. She took it outside and laid it on the ground next to the scattering of tools. Back at the table dealing with the short crust pastry, we watched from the window. For sure he would notice it. But what would he do? Would he ask any questions? If he did, she told me she'd be ready with her answer. 'I thought you'd like a little gift.' If he said nothing and put it into his toolbox, she'd have something to chide him about in the future, his dishonesty.

He spied it and, looking puzzled, glanced around, but no one was there and he'd just seen Mammy in the kitchen, up to her elbows in flour and margarine. Once he'd done the job, he put the tools in their respective places and found a slot for the mysterious Phillips screwdriver. He placed the box back on the top shelf in the cellar. Mammy had watched every move.

The police had to question men of around five feet five and who might fit the description of the person seen in Burnbank Street. Of course, it made sense to start locally and the name Adam Eden was eventually thrown up as a person of interest. I never knew if Mammy had a hand in drawing attention to Da but it wasn't long after that he told me how things turned out for him.

Mammy opened the door at ten o'clock on Saturday morning to two policemen who asked if Da was home. Iona and I strained our necks around the kitchen door to see what was going on. Da went to the door and invited them in; they wanted to speak with him in private. Mammy called on us and we made our way upstairs.

When they asked about his whereabouts on Monday past, he remembered her accusations from years ago when she thought he was a murderer. *Not again*, he thought.

From upstairs, we were told to keep quiet while Mammy strained her ears hoping the deep voices would carry, but all she could make out was 'toolbox' before she heard the back door open.

'What's wrong?' Iona asked.

Panic rose in Mammy before she sat back down on the bed. Trying to analyse what was going on, she fleetingly wondered if she'd made a huge mistake with the screwdriver.

'I don't know. Your da must have done something wrong.'

Da told me he didn't flinch when the police asked him about his hammers, chisels and wrenches. Finally, they focused on three screwdrivers. One policeman picked up on Da's hesitations and vague answer when he said he wasn't sure where they all came from. They needed some more information, so they invited him to the local police station for further questioning. The police told him he could call us downstairs.

Mammy had a smirk on her lips as Da walked calmly to the waiting patrol car. I heard her whisper, 'I wonder how he likes that?'

But her smugness didn't last long. Years ago, Mammy had hoped he'd be arrested for some crime and put away but, now that this was happening, she wasn't convinced that's what she needed to see. She voiced her feelings. Yes, she wanted him to squirm, but if he had to stay in a cell and couldn't go to work the following day, that would mean a loss of pay and her housekeeping would bear the brunt. And the neighbours, what must they be thinking?

As Mammy stared at the departing patrol car, the remaining policeman asked her to sit down. He explained that they needed to ask her some questions as well and were concerned that she might have felt intimidated if her husband was around.

'So why is all this happening?' she demanded.

'Let's start at the beginning,' he suggested. 'You will probably be aware of the serious incident that occurred on Monday when a man was attacked in his house on Burnbank Street.'

'Yes, well, I've heard some things, and I saw a bit in the paper, but that's all,' she replied. 'But why would you be interested in talking to my husband?'

The policeman avoided answering her directly. 'We're hoping he can help us with our inquiries. In the meantime, can you remember anything relating to your husband that occurred last Monday? Anything different from normal?'

Mammy rarely noted days and times, but she remembered that Da had arrived home slightly later than normal, probably after four o'clock. Iona had been earlier than him that day, which was unusual. She knew this because Iona had had the chance to grab a couple of biscuits and a bigger than normal glass of orange juice without being scolded. Da's standard line was always, 'You'll spoil your supper!' Iona tried to ignore his comments because nothing would spoil her appetite for food.

Da had gone directly upstairs, presumably to the toilet, without bothering to take off his long, black coat. Her memory of that had been triggered because of the strained discussion that had taken place a few weeks before about it smelling of smoke.

'Do you know where your husband keeps hammers and screwdrivers?' the policeman continued.

'In a toolbox, in the cellar.'

'OK, that can wait then. Thanks for your help.'

After he had gone, Mammy and Iona were right out into the cellar to have a look at the toolbox. This would be a great excuse to heave it down and see what treasures were inside. It was nowhere to be seen.

Meanwhile, Da was squirming. He felt trapped in the small interview room with two interrogators who were implying he was hiding information about the murdered man on Burnbank Street. He knew something serious was afoot and, in the pit of his stomach, felt Mammy was behind it. The interviewing policeman got a wealth of information.

It transpired that Da did not take kindly to men involved with one another. He viewed these kinds of relationships as abhorrent. Yes, he had delivered a tract to their house on Monday afternoon and yes; he remembered seeing two male names on the nameplate and tried to dismiss any visions he might have had of what might go on inside. He told the interviewer that even though the men had sinned, God would still forgive them, but clearly, he had a strong aversion to homosexuals.

Meanwhile, he couldn't explain how he had what appeared to be the partner of the screwdriver, which the police identified as the murder weapon. He fitted the description of a person of interest who had been seen at the door of the house on the afternoon of the murder. Da admitted he could have had good reason to have something to do with the crime. And he had the chance because he was in the area at the time. It appeared he was involved. Suddenly, everything fell into place for him.

He came clean and slapped his hands on the table. 'Wait!' He raised his hands, palms facing outwards, 'Listen, there's something I have to tell you. It's going to sound strange.'

The interviewer flipped his notebook open while the other policeman leaned forward and placed his hand on Da's arm. 'Go ahead, sir.'

It visibly relieved them, thinking they were about to get a confession, solve the case and get their paperwork written up.

It was a different confession that finally came. 'I am genuinely an honest man, but I am guilty of something that I think is confusing here.'

Da explained how he had discovered the screwdriver but didn't know where it came from. Finally, they told him he could pick up his toolbox the following day, but they kept the Phillips screwdriver.

After a few days, they found the culprit. Over a pint in the local, a neighbour overheard a drunk middle-aged man saying he could now live in peace because he had got rid of Joe. An anonymous phone call to the police spurred them into action and questions turned to accusations and finally an arrest. There was no need to pull anyone else in, and Da was no longer a suspect.

And so the truth emerged. A dispute between the neighbour and Joe had finally reached its peak on the Monday morning after the neighbour had been to a hardware shop to buy new screwdrivers. He heard Joe's radio blaring as he walked up the adjoining garden path. That set him off, and he complained about the noise that had come from Joe's television the night before. Everything got out of hand and the result was that he ripped open the packet and threatened Joe with a screwdriver.

'You're an auld moan. Get away from my door and get your nose out of my business,' Joe had shouted.

He took his threat a step further. Pushing past Joe, the neighbour stormed into the living room and turned Joe's radio off. Joe sat down, laughing for seconds before the culprit fixed a flat-head screwdriver solidly into the side of his skull. The neighbour had casually walked out of Joe's house, pulling the door closed behind him. He dropped the other screwdriver into a pile of snow.

Chapter 12

While all this had been going on, Da made a decision. He would accept the post of inspector for a trial period of three months. He and another colleague from the garage, Bob Scott, had been promoted at the same time. They still worked shifts but didn't have to follow a strict timetable; they made their own routes to look out for drivers who didn't adhere to their shift hours, buses not being on time, or incorrect tickets being issued. Being meticulous men, this seemed the perfect job for Bob and Da.

Inspectors wore similar uniforms to the drivers but were easily recognisable. Normally, Bob would wait at a stop along with the public, jump on the bus and have a general chit-chat with the driver. If the driver was early or late, a bit of banter followed with a friendly warning to be careful in the future. With the passengers' tickets checked; he might ask one or two people where they were going to make sure the conductor had recorded the correct destination and charged the right amount of money.

Da became a vigilante and, as well as making sure everything ran smoothly, he wanted to trap employees. He hid behind walls and bushes, waiting for the next bus so that he would catch the driver unaware; his serious attitude didn't go down well with the drivers and the conductors grew to dislike him.

He spoke to Bob confidentially to see if he had the same experiences. It transpired that there was an ulterior motive behind Bob accepting the job. He wanted to invest in his own bus company, so he needed to experience every part of the job to discover potential pitfalls. He knew the importance of keeping the men on his side to make sure they put in a good day's work; a different focus from Da's.

After his three-month trial period, I came home to find Da in the house alone and looking down in the mouth. Not that he was ever a happy, jolly man, but that day he appeared despondent.

'Hello, Alice.' His voice was flat.

'What's wrong?' I thought something might have happened to Mammy.

'I've decided not to continue as an inspector. The stress of the responsibility is dragging me down. I'm not a man who normally mixes with a lot of the workers at break times but since I've taken this job, I've been further isolated. Some men are sending me to Coventry.'

'What does that mean?'

'They ignore me completely! They don't like me.'

I had never felt sorry for my da until that moment. Here was a man who fought to be recognised in his work and it had backfired. In his home, he was belittled at every opportunity by Mammy. Although she wasn't entirely aware of what she was being roped into, Iona wasn't far behind in also belittling him. She and Mammy made up a force to be reckoned with.

I was changing my mind about Da being the evil, wicked man that Mammy made him out to be. Yes, he was blinkered in order to do right, as he saw it. I believe that's why adhering to a strict religious faith appealed to him. As much as was humanly possible, he took his commitment to God's word into every aspect of his life. There's no doubt he wouldn't have been an easy man to live or work with. He couldn't see the need to be flexible. In fact, he read that as being taken over, controlled, giving in and would have accused himself of being weak.

Apart from the mission, Da only had his family and his work. After battling at home for years, now those in his last place of respite were rejecting him.

He went back to driving, where his only obligation was to turn up for his shift. The men included him again.

Bob had asked Da to keep his enterprise plans a secret, which he did, and eventually, the new company started up in another city. Da felt he had been in a privileged position to have worked with and known such an astute business man. He boasted to anyone who would listen that Bob Scott was a close friend, an old buddy.

As chance would have it, Da bumped into Bob in a city department store a few months later. His business was going from strength to strength, and he intended to expand. Da suggested they should meet up again; in fact, he was bold enough to suggest he stop in to see Bob sometime. Bob agreed and gave Da his telephone number. He was happy he had crossed paths with his old mate again, but instinctively knew he wouldn't share this meeting with my mammy. She could be an embarrassment to Da and to me.

On the few occasions when we went out as a family, we cringed at her behaviour. Because Mammy wasn't a tall lady, it was difficult for her to find a comfortable chair at the right height. If her feet didn't touch the ground, her legs dangled unceremoniously and if they managed to reach the ground, she sat with her legs apart. That would have been OK if she had worn trousers, but trousers were unacceptable for women who attended the mission. No one mentioned it, but there wasn't a single person in the room who could have been at ease sitting opposite my mammy. There was rudeness to her habit, and it was difficult for us to tell if she knew how embarrassing it was for everyone. Only now and again, and if there was no one else in the room, Da indicated she should close her legs. She did, but only for a minute or two. Then they would slowly part and the view appeared again. It was an impossible, awkward situation. Humiliated, Da would make excuses not to socialise. That normally signalled an end to any potential friendships.

Likewise, Da embarrassed Mammy. If they accepted an invitation to lunch with family or some of the few friends they had, it didn't matter how the conversation started, it always ended with Da holding an open Bible, spouting off something about sinners and how those in the room needed to become born-again Christians. If they were already of the same faith, that would be even more reason for him to delve deeper into the scriptures, debate the finer points of God's word and compare interpretations between the old and new testaments. After an hour, it became tedious for the onlookers, but Da was relentless. Most people felt it was disrespectful to interrupt a conversation about the Lord, so normal talk ceased while my da dominated the rest of the visit. People considered it impolite to leave the room to go to the toilet and the best solution for us youngsters was to escape into another room before any religious discussion began. If there was a disagreement, the visit would often end on a sticky note.

Three years after Mammy's first operation to remove the growth, the recurring discomfort in the same place worried her and the whole exhausting process was repeated. Visits to the doctor, prescriptions for medication which never completely eased the pain, appointments for X-rays and a referral to the specialist meant she wasn't the strong housewife she used to be. Once again, she was admitted to hospital.

Granny visited the day before Mammy's second operation was to take place and I accompanied her to the ward. Mammy lay silent on the bed with a contorted face.

'Were you not taking your medicine?' Granny put her hand on the bed covers as she sat down.

'Take your hand away, Mam. I can feel the bed moving. I can't take anything because the operation is tomorrow.'

'So, what are they saying it is?'

'I don't know,' was all Mammy could manage to say before closing her eyes again and clenching her teeth.

All she knew was that the growth had come back. In those days, everyone avoided words like tumour and cancer; even the medical staff. It wasn't unusual for the patient to be kept in the dark.

Following her operation, she had radiotherapy treatment sessions, so Da's car was a great help when she needed shopping. It was never on the cards that she should learn to drive; Da wouldn't have encouraged that. So the car sat in the driveway most of the time, because he seldom took it to work.

As the weeks went by, he took time for him and Mammy to explore more of the local area. She didn't normally plan anything for each second Saturday, hoping for a trip out after his early shift, but he started to make excuses about not going out for the Saturday run. He said he was tired after working or he'd need to fill up with petrol, which wouldn't leave much time for a day out. Or perhaps it looked like it was about to rain. More often than not, she didn't feel up to going out, so he went on his own to visit his family in Glasgow. However, Da really tried to be around to take Mammy food shopping. Days out had been highlights, but she told me she was disappointed when she couldn't face a trip or he made other arrangements; a reminder that things were just as they used to be. As she saw it, he was in control and she was at his mercy.

Da told me in confidence that now and again, he needed a break and a distraction from our home life. One Saturday afternoon, on his way back from Sam's house and within a few miles of Bob's, he stopped at a phone box and rang the number he had covertly protected for months. Bob's wife, Sarah, answered. Da was more than welcome to stop in for a cuppy. When he pulled his Mini into the driveway behind Bob's Range Rover, Da felt he had made it in life. How lucky he was to have friends who were so successful.

The men caught up with the news, then Sarah asked more about Da's background and family. He told them about the grocery shop and dairy he'd had and how these were no longer viable. His background impressed Sarah, and she mentioned she didn't realise he had owned businesses; like Bob. When Da was telling me this, he swelled with pride to be put in the same category as a prosperous business owner. Before he could divulge more about his wife and two children, Sarah left the room to answer the door. When Bob heard voices, he jumped up to welcome Sarah's best friend, Liz; she lit up the room when she strode in. The tall, forty-five-year-old redhead was holding a paper bag out in front of her.

'I know how to get a cup of tea out of these two. I bring my own doughnuts!' She laughed.

Da stood up and extended his hand as Bob formally introduced them.

'So, what's happening here? Are you keeping secrets from me?' Liz nodded towards my da.

'You're a cheeky monkey!' Bob poked fun at her. 'You're never away from here, so how could we have any secrets from you?'

They spent an enjoyable hour together until Da had to leave. The usual goodbye banter ensued, with a strong invitation for him to join them in a couple of weeks for Sarah's birthday. Da assured them he would try his best, but deep down, he knew it would be impossible. A party where there would likely be alcohol and frivolity was not his scene. Although he had enjoyed their company, he would come up with a good excuse to avoid the celebration. As Bob walked him down the path to his car, Sarah popped her head out of the living room window.

'Adam, just to say. When you come on my birthday, please don't bring a present. I don't need or want anything. And don't bring a bottle; we're all teetotal, so it would just be a waste of money.' She smiled and waved as she closed the window.

His attitude changed. He became animated and thought to himself the birthday get together might be a wonderful idea after all. He would be on an early shift that day. Yes, he would rub shoulders again with his prosperous friends.

Two days before the get together, he mentioned in passing to Mammy that he would go to see Sam after he'd finished his shift on Saturday. He said not to bother making him lunch, he'd come home, change, collect the car and head off.

'OK,' she said. 'That's good that I know, because I can make other plans. I might jump on the bus and go into town if I feel like it, or I might visit Madge.'

But his announcement reminded Mammy that the car wasn't a family car, it was *his* car. She still had to scurry around the shops and trail home with shopping bags when she was able.

She was mad and spoke her mind to me one evening when I dared to sit on the red and grey chair. Iona was in bed and Mammy needed to get things off her chest. There was no doubt she wanted to scupper Da's enjoyment of the car. But, she knew even if she could get into the engine, she wouldn't have a clue what to do to cause mischief. The idea of a flat tyre appealed to her; she needed to disable the car. Anything less, such as a scrape along the side, wouldn't stop him in his tracks. She had to find out how a puncture might happen and, as luck would have it, a conversation on that very topic came up between her and the couple next door.

Their son had been driving on a country road when he felt the steering wheel pulling to one side. When he got out to check the car, he had a flat tyre and was stuck in the middle of nowhere with his wife and baby for over an hour until an emergency vehicle rescued them. The garage discovered a nail had caused the problem. Mammy found out the tyre had an inner tube, much like a bicycle, and a long enough piece of glass or a nail could penetrate the outer thick rubber part and possibly puncture the inner tube.

On Thursday evening, Da walked down to the mission and Mammy set about putting her plan in motion. She was sure he wouldn't take the car to work the next morning; he'd said before that he liked the early morning stroll. With it parked on their side driveway, she could tamper with it out of sight of the neighbours. She had to get out before it became too dark. By nine o'clock, the sun would be well down and Da would be on his way home after the prayer meeting,

The minute he left the house, she gathered her garden trowel, fork and the newly sharpened garden shears. Although she was feeling under the weather, she knelt on a small cushion and pretended to weed part of the flower bed running alongside the concrete slabs that formed the driveway. Even as she was mixing up the soil, her eye was on the wheel nearest to her. She caught sight of the deeper grooves as she laid the shears down. After pottering around for a few minutes, she delved into her pocket and pulled out a long nail, rammed the point into the deep groove on one of the front tyres with the handle of the trowel and waited. Nothing happened, so she turned back to her weeding, leaving the nail where it was. After all that, she was certain her plan wouldn't work. She leaned forward and levelled off the patch of earth, accidentally kicking the shears; they hit against the nail but didn't dislodge it. She picked up the garden tools and her little bag of weeds, hopeful that the nail would eventually damage the tyre.

Early on Friday morning, as expected, Da walked to work. Later, Mammy took a bus to the shops and popped in to see Madge. Around three o'clock, as she turned the corner towards home, she noticed the driveway was empty. She thought Da must have arrived home early then gone out in the car for something. In the few minutes it took to get to the front door, different scenarios flitted through her mind. She imagined him driving off then getting to the road end when the tyre would start to deflate; she smirked when she thought of how annoyed and inconvenienced he would be, not only for that day but also for the entire weekend. Then she thought he might have got further than the road end and picked up speed on the busier road that led towards the mission; she paled as it struck her that the car might have skidded off the road. Suddenly, the picture in her mind was of laughing children on the pavement and mothers pushing their babies in prams while the Mini careered towards them. Trying not to visualise the horror of what might have taken place, her trembling hands got the key in the lock. She heard voices. Peering into the living room, she saw my da in his chair while another man, a stranger, sat on the couch; both were drinking tea. Mammy stared at Da, who forced a weak smile at her.

'Oh, hello.' Her voice was shaky.

The stranger placed his cup and saucer on the coffee table and stood up.

'Hello, I take it you're Mrs Eden? I'm Bill Jones; I live a couple of streets away.' The man stood up and Mammy accepted his extended hand.

She took her coat off but held onto it; having something in her hands seemed to steady their trembling. She remained standing.

Bill explained he had crossed the main road about an hour beforehand when Da's Mini approached the traffic lights. Out of the corner of his eye, he noticed it was veering towards the middle of the road then weaving its way back towards the pavement. He knew something was wrong and shouted to warn two people walking on the pavement. Fortunately, the car stopped before it was anywhere near the couple and Da was OK. Bill stepped in to help and called a garage from a nearby phone box. No one was injured, only the car was out of commission with a burst tyre, but it was in the garage as they spoke.

Immediately, Mammy's shaking became more visible. Her face was white by this time, her legs trembled, and her bottom lip moved up and down, with no sound emanating from her mouth.

'I can't believe it.' She managed a few words.

Da bent over to lay his cup down and stayed leaning forward, staring at her. She sounded as though she cared. But it was relief that had flooded through Mammy, relief that nothing more serious had come from her stupid prank. Da got up and made the unusual move of putting the kettle on for the second time that day. The conversation became bizarre when Bill smiled and nodded.

'I know you're worried about your husband,' he said with concern. 'I can see how troubled you are. He's shaken, but now that I've seen how upset you are, I'm sure he's in excellent hands.' He stood up to go. 'I wish my wife was as worried about me. She would have been hoping I'd have come out the worst in a situation like this!' He had a twinkle in his eye and the hint of a smile on his lips.

When Da saw Bill to the door, Mammy finally sat down to drink her tea. Once her trembling stopped, she picked up her coat and sighed as she hung it up.

'Right,' she announced. 'I suppose I'd better peel the potatoes now that you're still here.'

She wondered if he detected the bitter irony in her comment.

Da collected the car later that day, paid for the repair and drove home. The mechanics showed him what they'd found. It confused him how he had run over such a long nail and reckoned it must have been sticking up between paving stones or broken kerb stones somewhere. He now had the car back for his clandestine get-together the following day.

Sam and Jen welcomed Da the next afternoon; he had little time to spare before he was due at Bob's. While he was telling me this, I could hear the excitement in his voice as he relived that Saturday. It surprised Jen when he politely refused the usual cuppy before darting upstairs to the spare room where his emergency clothes hung on two hangers. He reached into the wardrobe for his dark brown flannel trousers, crisp white shirt with tie, and the sports jacket he hadn't worn for many a month. He dressed, then almost skipped downstairs in his socks. He held his shoes out and asked if by any chance he could borrow some brown shoe polish. Like an excited teenager, he was off to mix with his new friends at the type of social gathering he had only dreamt of before.

The uneventful journey to Bob's took just over half an hour, and the traffic was quiet. He had time to reflect on how great a day it had been so far and thought about who he might encounter. He also had time to stop off to buy a bunch of flowers. For the second time, he pulled in behind Bob's Range Rover and breathed deeply, attempting to quell his eagerness.

Bob answered the door. 'Hah! Speak of the devil!' Da welcomed his warm handshake. 'Hey, Sarah. We've got a well-dressed young man here! Come in! Come in! Glad you could make it, Adam.'

Laughter and voices rose from inside. Strains of soft music drifted in the background and the air was filled with a delicate fragrance. Da had followed Bob into the living room where Sarah and Liz were sitting on the red leather Chesterfield. He greeted them both before Sarah jumped up. Da wished her a happy birthday and her jaw dropped when he handed her the flowers.

'Adam, that's far too much! They're beautiful! Oh, how did you know lilies were my favourite?'

Bob introduced Da to Issy and her husband Ted, then offered him a seat. Once they dispensed with the usual pleasantries, the whole affair became relaxed and jovial. He told me they served tea, along with a scrumptious selection of mini sandwiches, scones, and cakes. Da sat next to Liz at the table and listened intently to what the small group's backgrounds were. He was more than interested when Liz spoke about the tearoom she owned on the banks of a loch. The hours passed until Da said his goodbyes, after agreeing to visit again soon. Liz and Sarah saw him to the door and waved goodbye as his little car drove off into the dusky evening.

Da couldn't shake Liz and her tearoom from his mind. He admired her dedication to the business and, from the conversation he'd had with her, she sounded like an astute business woman; a rare commodity in his eyes.

'A woman! With a business! My, my. What is the world coming to? Next we'll have women driving buses.' He laughed and shook his head as he turned onto the main road.

Within the month, he made sure he was in the area Liz had mentioned. Her description and direction had been spot on. He saw the row of six shops with the tearoom at the end. There were four wrought-iron tables with chairs outside and a low, white picket fence surrounded the patio. A young couple sipped cold drinks at one table. Da had parked the Mini nearby, strolled up as casually as he could, and opened the patio gate. The place looked welcoming. Liz was clearing a wooden table when the tinkle of the bell alerted her to a new customer.

'Adam! How are you?' Her face glowed.

'Hello, Liz. I was passing and remembered my promise to come in.'

'Well, I'm glad you did! Sit down.' She gestured to a table near the window, then peered through a hatch into the kitchen area. 'Helen, will you make sure the fruit loaves come out of the oven? They must be ready now.'

The tearoom wasn't busy inside; the only remaining customers were a family of three and a couple sorting out their money.

'Adam, let me get you tea and give me five minutes. I'm due a break, so I'll join you once I get Helen sorted.'

And that's exactly what she did. The place looked ordered and clean, so, with Helen in charge of the till and the teapot, Liz sat down. Half an hour passed before she saw her colleague needed a hand but, in that time, Da and Liz had made a connection.

He found out she had never married, had no family of her own, although she deemed her Sunday school class to be her children. She sang in the church choir and lived with her sister and brother-in-law while waiting to move into her new flat. She'd built the tearoom up from an old greasy-spoon café to what it was now. Most of the soft furnishings were her own handiwork, but she couldn't do more serious repairs. The only things outstanding were a boiler that needed to be built in and a couple of broken tables out the back. Da had a look. No problem to him, a would-be carpenter. He was overjoyed that someone might appreciate his work. He assured Liz that the next time he came, he would be armed with a measuring tape, a few tools and plenty of time.

On the drive home, Da said he had reflected on our family, work and his future. Although he enjoyed the company of his new friends, he wasn't sure if he was doing the right thing in the eyes of God. He had thought about how disillusioned he was with Mammy's awkward ways and uncontrollable temper. Now, by the looks of things after two operations, she was facing a tough time, but we all had to grin and bear it. His relationship with her had been a struggle, but she was his wife; sacred matrimony meant staying with what he had. Work-wise, he was a plodder these days; he had lost the desire to branch out and make something of his dormant business ideas. He tried to keep calm and healthy, to be part of the workforce and earn a living. As for the future, he dismissed any ideas of change. His new friends were wonderful company with warm personalities, but he decided right there and then. There was no time for diversions if he was to support Mammy, so he put Bob, Sarah, and Liz to the back of his mind.

Da knew he could be a serious man, and that others laughed more than he did. He had moments of reminiscing about life and his horrific war experiences. The bombing, losing friends, and dealing with unimaginable casualties all continued to haunt him. When he had tried to buck himself up and start a business, a marriage and a life, he could never have imagined that constant goading from Mammy, the one who he had loved dearly, would add to his tension and worry.

Once Da was out working or visiting his family, Mammy had absolutely no qualms about blackening his character to me. She felt I was old enough at sixteen to listen to what she thought about him. She never subjected ten-year-old Iona to this, but Mammy spent hours dragging up the past to me, spouting out her hatred for him and for the things he did or didn't do.

Whenever the opportunity arose for me and my mammy to be in the living room alone, the conversation would start. I didn't mind initially, but eventually, these talks became repetitive and tiresome. I sometimes sat opposite her on the red and grey chair with my eyelids slowly closing, only for them to jerk open again after a few seconds. I wasn't rude enough to leave her in mid-sentence, especially if she was on a roll, but I often wished Mammy had someone else to speak to. I couldn't solve her problems and I wasn't sure if that's really what she was looking for.

One evening while Da was working and Iona was in bed, Mammy began the usual ranting about how she was sure he had been involved in the disappearances of children and the murders of young women. She ruminated again about the early days of her marriage and how she couldn't understand Da's attitude to life, his frugality, his secretiveness, his need to control everything. He was a boring man who didn't match up to the excitement she had hoped for.

Mammy had been fun and usually up for a laugh, but now she was despondent and not only blamed my da for her depressive moods but also for the stress he caused, which, she believed, had resulted in her illness. In the early days of their relationship, she had coaxed him out of his serious mood, but over the years that had become hard work and she had stopped trying long ago. Now, Da saw most fun as pointless. He reminded her every day of the things he wanted to happen. Put this here, don't leave that there, and always questioning why she bought certain things. Since he had had his ulcer operation many years ago, every meal or snack was preceded by him reminding her not to put certain foods anywhere near his plate and not to cut his sandwiches with a knife she used for food he couldn't eat.

As I sat listening, I was repeatedly told that Da wasn't the good man he purported to be. To back up her perception of him, Mammy told me of a time when he had come back on leave from the army. He had stayed in Granny's house with the family, including Aunt Jane, who was a teenager. The story went, Mammy walked into a bedroom and found Da and Aunt Jane in a compromising position. She closed the door and left them to it. It was a shock to me to be told my principled, religious father had had a clandestine relationship with Mammy's younger sister. Then she went on.

'You won't remember this, but when you were about three years old, your da used to watch you now and again while I went out to the women's meeting at the church. You were always sleeping by the time I got home. One morning when he went to work, you told me that the night before, when he put you to bed, he said he was going to put a big stick in your tummy and make it all wet.'

I stopped in my tracks. At sixteen, I knew what she was referring to.

'But, as a wee girl, you were OK about it; you just kind of dismissed it after you had told me the story then asked if you could play with your dolls in the bath.'

My mind was reeling.

'And can you believe it? The same thing happened with Iona years later when she was the same age. But her reaction was different from yours. She was crying the next morning and tried to tell me how she felt. It was the same story with the same words. She wanted to stay close to me for days after that.'

I wasn't brave enough to ask the questions that were forming in my head. Had I been more alert, I would have wanted to say: If my da had done that to me, why didn't you report it? Did you ever leave me with him again? How would you know this would never happen in the future? And why years later would you have left him with Iona? Am I meant to believe that he did this to her when I was nine years old and could have caught him? If you reported him for thinking he was murdering people in Glasgow, why would you not alert the authorities if he was abusing his two young daughters? If you wanted to destroy this man at every turn, are you telling me you kept this to yourself and didn't expose him for doing something that would have brought him to his knees?

After the allegations, I was disgusted. Mammy's revelations had come at a crucial point in my education and development as a young lady. I felt I couldn't look at, never mind talk to Da again. The following afternoon, I gathered my things for a sleepover with two friends and, as I started down the stairs, I encountered him nearing the turn at the top; I glared disgust into his face as I stormed past.

Taken aback, he whispered, 'Oh, Alice!'

What Mammy didn't know was that the man who had retreated into the corner at the stair turn didn't have to think very hard about who was responsible for my reaction to him. What was more of a puzzle was the why.

I left the house without saying much more than a general goodbye.

Da had watched Mammy and Iona carefully, waiting for any other unusual reactions, but none came and the three of them sat down to eat. When he enquired about me, Mammy told him I was at a friend's house. She didn't volunteer any more information. Years later, he admitted he silently hoped he had been mistaken about the look of hate from me. Plus, there was nothing concrete to back up his suspicion that Mammy was involved, so he put it down to something she must have prevented me from doing earlier.

For weeks afterwards, Da was aware of me doing everything I possibly could to avoid being within six feet of him. When he tried to speak to me, I was decidedly frosty in my replies. He knew there was more to this story, and the smugness he sensed in my mammy confirmed his earlier fears. She was involved for sure and he was discerning enough to know that she wouldn't be happy with just an atmosphere between him and me. She would be forced to blurt it out eventually, but he would have to bide his time before he knew more.

Mammy was, understandably, preoccupied with her health. She often sat alone in the living room and wondered what the point was of buying anything to make her life more comfortable. Barely on her feet again after her second operation, within the year the bad news astounded her; the treatment was not working and a third operation loomed. Mammy had to endure more surgery, followed by radiotherapy.

Once home, she didn't have the strength or inclination to deal with petty incidents, though she never missed an opportunity to disparage Da. This time, her weakened system and spirit were clear.

I was aware of Mammy lying on the couch or sitting around more, although not always reliving the past, certainly not forgetting that Da had riddled her life with disappointment. It partly focused her mind when she made sure she attended to her health by changing her diet and trying to live as stress-free an existence as possible. But there was an inherent bitterness that caused her to lash out with accusations from recreated scenes in her mind. Maybe feeling she was running out of time, Mammy maligned Da's character to Iona with the same stories she'd told me, even passing on the tale that Da had abused us when we were three years old.

Her attempt to plant false memories failed dramatically. To me, these accounts were without substance because nothing ever came of the allegations. I couldn't remember anything that would have even hinted at abuse.

I watched as Iona clung to Mammy while she was recovering post-surgery; she helped with simple chores or trips to the local shop. She was usually rewarded with a bar of chocolate, but that's not why she did it. Iona was a natural at caring for Mammy. Not quite a teenager yet, she fussed around her. On days when Mammy was feeling weak and took to her bed, Iona would climb in beside her. To a certain extent, Mammy used Iona as a counsellor but never to the same degree that she had with me. Iona could escape from the grey and red chair when she pointed out that she still had homework to do or had to get up extra early the following morning.

Chapter 13

Granny arrived at our house and gave Mammy the news that Billy, Georgie and Rose's son from Australia, was to visit Scotland the following month and would like to see as many of the family as possible. This was the first contact Mammy would have with her nephew in many years. There had been little news of Georgie and his family after they had left almost fifteen years before, although my granny had visited Australia three times. Da was never told about Billy's upcoming visit because of the unresolved issues with his parents from the time at the grocer's shop.

Billy couldn't remember much of his Aunt Chris and she was tearful when she saw what a handsome, successful young man he had become. She had missed out on many years with that side of her family, all because Da was frugal, unrelenting. The strictness of his religious principles had made it hard for him to be flexible and understanding of others all these years ago, and he had never changed.

Describing life in Australia, Billy assured Mammy that his father had no regrets about moving. When the family had relocated, it was thanks to a deal whereby families could go for the princely sum of £10 if the breadwinner had secured a job and had an address to give the authorities. Distant relatives of our family were already in Melbourne, so Georgie had taken advantage of the offer. He had said he had nothing left in Scotland after his business dealings with Da had fallen through.

Mammy regretted not having had the chance to say goodbye to them all these years ago; it was something she harboured but didn't dare make her feelings known to Da. As far as he was concerned, Georgie had betrayed him and he wouldn't get another chance. That he had moved to the other side of the world was a bonus in Da's eyes.

Mammy put her brother's address in a safe place, promising Billy she would at least write a letter. With a faraway look in her eyes, she told me about now having a way to contact Georgie and not having to rely on getting news from Granny.

Billy had seen his Aunt Chris was frail and asked me if she would ever recover. I didn't want to think as far ahead as that. He made his way back to Australia satisfied he had seen what he could of his extended family.

A few weeks passed before Mammy contacted Georgie; she bought some airmail writing paper and envelopes. Questions might be raised about these if Da had found them, so she instigated a conversation with him about her Aunt Jemima in America. Granny had already visited Jemima in New York and brought back stories of a wonderful life there. Mammy said she intended to write to her aunt.

But when she had the right words, she started her letter to Georgie by explaining her health situation. Three operations and a drawn-out recovery had dominated her everyday life, but she tried to convince herself she was getting stronger. She wrote about life in the new town in Scotland and how the girls were growing fast. She told him she had very much enjoyed Billy's brief visit and hoped she could someday visit Melbourne.

She didn't include her address at the top but asked him to contact Granny if he intended to reply; she daren't risk a letter arriving at the house from Australia. Da would have been furious at her disloyalty and may well have opened it. He was good at finding excuses for that sort of behaviour. He could say he thought it was something for him; she remembered she had done exactly that with the dreaded bank book a few years before. He might take the letter and destroy it without her knowledge or even write 'No longer at this address' on the envelope and hope that it would wing its way back to the sender.

Out of the blue, a few weeks later, I arrived home to hear that Granny had arrived and spent a few hours with Mammy while we were at school. It happened Da was on a back shift, so mother and daughter could sit and chat the entire afternoon without fear of interruption. Granny said she'd had a letter from Australia with news that Georgie and Rose had split up, but he had acknowledged receipt of Mammy's letter.

'He says you're going to visit him?' Granny quizzed.

'Well, I'd like to, but you know what it's like here. Adam wouldn't go and I don't know if it's something I could do on my own. I couldn't take the girls, they've got school. Anyway, I don't think I'd ever be able to afford a ticket for myself, never mind the three of us,' she responded with a downcast look.

Granny had jumped in. 'I did it. Three times. There are people to help every step of the way. It's a long journey, so you can't just go for a week; you'd need to stay for at least a month to make it worth your while. But you'd need to speak to the doctors. Do you think you'd be able to stand the travelling?'

She tried to be encouraging, but appreciated Mammy had her work cut out if she ever wanted to move further than her front door. She had a disciplinarian of a husband, not to mention some serious health issues.

Mammy only spoke of her dream to me. Iona was never to know, as somehow she couldn't trust her youngest with her secret longing. But that wasn't the only reason. Mammy felt reality was hitting her, and she was scared to think that she wouldn't survive her illness. The doctor had said that she needed to be positive and plan.

I knew my mammy kept Uncle Georgie's address in her drawer; Mammy and Da had their own drawers in the upstairs bedroom and neither was to be opened by anyone else without permission. That rule had been in place for many years but, although Iona claimed she had never opened them, she miraculously knew what was in each drawer. If Mammy needed a pen or a necklace from upstairs, she would send one of us, normally Iona, to retrieve it. That never happened with Da; his drawer was completely forbidden territory.

One day, Mammy asked Iona to go upstairs to get a magnifying glass which should have been in the right-hand side of her drawer. Da was in the bedroom when Iona burst in, opened Mammy's drawer, and rummaged.

He eventually relayed the story of how he came to know of the communication between Mammy and her brother. I think Da couldn't believe his luck the day Iona opened the drawer; then he could see what Mammy kept there. He had leapt over to Iona's side to scold her for making a mess. But, he spied a small piece of white paper; all he could make out with a brief glance was 'Melbourne, Australia' written on it. Iona brushed off his reprimand, picked up the now uncovered magnifying glass, slammed the drawer shut and darted down the stairs.

Da knew he only had a moment. He opened Mammy's drawer, didn't touch a thing but memorised what he needed to from the now visible white paper with an Australian address and confined it to memory. He only needed to remember three things: the number, the street name, and the district. After repeating it to himself twice, he had it. There hadn't been a name on the paper, but he made an educated guess it was to do with Georgie.

Mammy eventually rearranged her drawer and found a new hiding place for the address in a hatbox beside a special red purse and a gold ring that needed the setting fixed.

It dawned on Da that the airmail stationery he had seen in the drawer in the living room might be connected to the nameless Australian address. As soon as he could, he recovered the writing pad. The white card that was supposed to be placed between the flimsy sheets of blue-lined airmail paper had been removed. He tore out the top page.

The next day at work, he found a quiet corner in the canteen and brought out the blank page. Just as he'd hoped, there was an impression of what she had written on the previous page. The words weren't clear, especially on the right-hand side where the pen had done its job without applying too much pressure, but he could decipher most of it.

... now that I'm feeling much stronger, it would be ....
and see you. If you could tell me when you and ....
be the best time I will find out about tickets. You ....
on my own. Can you write to Mammy and she will ....
airport. I can't come by ship as Mammy did because ....
Give my love to Rose if you see her and I hope this ....
From Chris.

Da was shocked. His instincts had been right; Mammy was not only communicating with the man who had practically ruined his grocery business, but she was also making plans to visit him. To visit Australia! He wiped his mouth with the back of his hand and saw blood; he was so angry he hadn't felt his teeth sink into his bottom lip. If he had been in any place other than the works canteen, he would have chucked the dark blue mug across the room. He said his head was reeling, and he knew he needed time to think things through. In an overly controlled manner, he packed his bits and pieces into his haversack, took the mug back to the counter, and strode out into the bright sunlight to walk home.

By the end of the week, and despite Da being convinced Mammy's illness was too far gone for recovery, he began discussing rehabilitation and convalescence. He asked if she'd ever thought of going anywhere else; if there was somewhere she felt she could travel to. She told him maybe not at that precise moment, but she could go away in the future if Iona and I would help at home now that we were growing up.

It all fell into place for Mammy. She told me about the conversation with Da and said that she had secretly thought she might be able to make the journey to see Georgie in a month or two. She smiled as she thought about her first steps.

'I'm going to ask the travel agents next week about Australia,' she announced purposefully as she straightened the front of her pale green quilted housecoat, 'but I'm not telling anyone, so don't you say a word. I'm determined I'm going to get better and I'm not having any more operations. They've told me there's different treatment if I need it.'

Another week passed, and I came home to see a smiling mammy.

'Madge told me the travel agent said there's a special offer that ends next Friday.' Mammy beamed at me. 'It's because it's coming into winter in Australia and I can get it practically at half-price. I want to do it. I'm going to do it!'

'Wow, that's quick! Where will you get the money?' I asked, screwing up my brows. I thought this was a flash in the pan; it would never happen.

'I have a bit put aside. If you and Iona think you can cope, all I have to do now is tell him.' She jerked her thumb toward the back door.

On Thursday, Mammy struggled into town and put down a small deposit on her dream holiday. She had an appointment the next day at the hospital to set up dates for a course of treatment. She would have to stay in hospital for three days at a time over the next couple of months and wasn't looking forward to it, but the idea of getting better and thoughts of Australia lifted her spirits.

It wasn't long before Mammy took a turn for the worse. She couldn't make it to the first appointment for treatment, so the doctor came in and prescribed extra-strong painkillers. Da understood the seriousness of Mammy's illness; I felt I knew, but Iona was oblivious to how critical her state of health was. Dr Davidson said that, under normal circumstances, a patient would take three painkillers a day but, given that Mammy had lost her appetite and was fading, he suggested Da should leave the bottle on the bedside cabinet to let her administer them herself.

The doctor could see there was nothing else that could be done for Mammy and it was time to let her decide her fate; he was suggesting that if the pills were left nearby, she could take them all at once rather than prolonging the agony of such a devastating illness. Da refused. He was going to give her the tablets when he thought she should have them. By this time, Mammy was fragile in body and spirit and didn't care that he was controlling things right to the end.

Finally, I realised my mammy's impending demise was imminent. Da had spelled it out to me when it was clear from the way she looked. With clumps replacing what had been a healthy mop of curly brown hair and much thinner limbs, there was no chance of recovery. We were preparing ourselves for the worst, yet Mammy's odd comments and questions about her health were met with avoidance or denial from us. That was the way things were in those days. But she was also avoiding things. I asked her what the big lump on her head was, only to be told it was when she had bumped it going into the car. I knew she hadn't been in the car for weeks, but I didn't realise this was the cancer spreading and taking over every part of her body.

The speed at which her already frail body was disappearing let us know the cancer had beaten her. Within days, she was staring at everyone with sunken eyes and there was no hair left on her head. Her saddened mouth took on a more resigned shape in her shrunken face. No longer was her voice firm; it was clear that she had no strength left to utter more than a few words now and again. She refused any type of food. Of course she had lost some weight over the five years since her first operation, but the culmination of the visible signs told everyone, including Mammy herself, that it was the end. Da, the man who had seen death many times during the war and several times in his personal life, knew his wife didn't have long to live.

He took time off his work and was there when the ambulance came to pick Mammy up in late January. Except for Da and me, she didn't have visitors in her single hospital room. The doctors told us there was very little hope that she would survive more than a few days. The change in her was rapid as she drifted in and out of a dream world. Although she wasn't eating, one afternoon Da had brought an orange. He stood beside her bed and peeled off a few segments. Holding one firmly, he leaned over and put it to Mammy's mouth so that she could get some liquid. She sucked on it with vigour as I looked on. My legs involuntarily took a step back.

It was as though I was intruding on something that shouldn't involve me. Mammy and Da were close, physically and mentally. He was helping her; she was accepting it. In an instant, I saw kindness, maybe even love, flit between them as she stared at him and he stared back.

I thought you hated each other?

The words flashed through my mind as I retreated from their private moment. I looked out of the window at the trees waving in the February wind, pointing towards the heavens, and felt deep compassion for my mammy who was now rambling.

'How can I go with all these people around and that wee boy down there?'

I turned back towards her. Da turned away, and it was me who answered, 'It's all right, Mammy. We'll find a way.'

Then we left for home.

Whether she had been dreaming of Australia or simply hallucinating, we never knew because she slipped away the next day, in the early hours of 2nd February.

Da had slept on the couch that night. He was expecting news. The police came to the house to tell him of Mammy's passing about six in the morning. The knock on the door had disturbed me, but it was Da who finally wakened me. I followed him downstairs to hear the news. He gave me the job of telling Iona, who opened her eyes as I leaned over her sleeping frame and whispered her name.

'Iona, I'll give you a second or two to wake up, but I have something to tell you.'

'Oh, OK. I think I know what you're going to say.' Iona looked at me sitting on the edge of her bed.

'Mammy won't be coming home from hospital. She went to heaven this morning,' I said as I took my sister's hand.

Iona cried; she had lost her soulmate. I kept it together until I was alone.

There were formalities to be carried out. A friend looked after Iona while I went with Da on the day of Mammy's passing to do what was necessary. A few minutes after we had left the house by car, we saw a neighbour walking home. Da asked me to roll down the car window and tell her the news. It seemed odd to me. Was that the way my mammy's death was to be announced? He slowed the car down and the neighbour approached. I got the window half down, but no words came out of my mouth; I put my head in my hands and sobbed.

'Oh!' Da leaned across me and spoke through the open passenger window to the woman. 'It's just to tell you that Chris died this morning.'

The neighbour put her hand to her mouth, shook her head, and walked away.

'I'm sorry Alice, I didn't realise…' Da spoke with a hint of concern.

What he didn't grasp was that I was shocked at the excitement in his voice. He sounded pleased to pass on the news; he couldn't hide the fact that he wasn't a grieving husband.

Losing Mammy devastated me and Iona, but there was relief that she was no longer ravaged by such a brutal illness. Da planned with the funeral directors to leave the casket open, but he was the only one who viewed her until the day of the funeral.

A few friends gathered for the service, Madge and Bert, along with some people from the mission, including Mr and Mrs Hyde. Our Aunt Jane was there along with Granny, as were some of Da's family, Sam and Jen, and his other brother, Grant. Da approached each person to say that the casket, which was in a private room, was about to be closed, so this was the last opportunity to view my mammy. He invited me in. I had never seen a dead body before, but I had to go in because I would never see her again.

'Do you think Iona would like to come in?' Da asked.

I walked outside to where Iona was sitting alone and knelt down beside her.

'You know you don't have to, but Da was wondering if you'd like to see Mammy.'

'No! No!' Iona shook her head emphatically. 'But can I ask you one thing? Can I have her wedding ring?'

Her request dumbfounded me because Mammy's marriage hadn't been memorable for its happiness, but then I realised that Mammy never took her wedding ring off for any reason. She sometimes left her engagement ring in her bedroom, but the wedding ring was an important part of Mammy. Da agreed and asked the undertaker to remove it. He handed it to Iona, and she immediately put it on her middle finger.

In front of the family and a few friends in a cemetery on the outskirts of Falkirk, we laid Mammy to rest. Granny stood at her daughter's graveside, tight-lipped. Her happy baby girl had grown up to be an unhappy and unfulfilled woman, and now it was all over.

Da had suggested Jen sing a special hymn at the graveside; he felt it was an appropriate way to remind the mourners that, as he believed, the grave does not have victory and death is all part of God's plan.

The few rushed words from the pastor signalled the end when heavy raindrops fell on his open Bible.

'Yea, though I walk through the valley of the shadow of death, I will fear no evil: for thou art with me; thy rod and thy staff, they comfort me. Amen.'

The rain poured down with a vengeance. It was as though the elements were preventing Mammy from getting the recognition she wanted, even in her ultimate resting place. Our group broke up quicker than expected to avoid getting soaked, but Aunt Jane hung back and stood by my side.

'I can't believe that woman could stand there and sing.' Aunt Jane was more familiar with traditional funerals; weeping, grieving, and mourning. It wasn't conventional to involve singing and giving thanks for a life, but that was part of Da's religious beliefs. Jane wiped away her tears. 'These people don't know, but your mammy and da were really happy at one time.'

I knew that. There was a bond between them that was warped because of guilt borne of religion. I grieved for more than Mammy's physical passing; I felt deep sorrow for the waste of a life, of all of our lives, because of Mammy's fundamental desire to destroy Da.

When the time was right, Da asked me to help arrange a tombstone, but it didn't carry the same sentiments as most of the others that stood in lines in the graveyard. There was no 'sadly missed' or 'in loving memory'. It read:

To the memory of Christina Eden.

As the weeks turned into months, Da was thankful that he had peace in his life, but he was lonely. To a certain extent, he had been a lonely man all his life; Mammy had made sure of that.

As the next couple of years passed, we girls muddled through as best we could, but Da's strictness about where we could go and when we had to come back created uneasiness in the house.

I left school; I secured a job doing secretarial work in a local insurance office. That didn't satisfy me, so I finally applied for jobs in the city and moved into a small flat. I left home for good and visits back home diminished as I built up a new circle of friends.

Da looked after the house with very little help from Iona. He ensured she ate and had a roof over her head, but it was a cold, lonely place without a mother. Iona spent more and more time at friends' houses and bonded closely with one special person, Sally. Every second weekend on his late shifts, Da arranged for Iona to stay over at Sally's house. She was delighted, and he was also free to go to visit his family. Secretly, he had hoped to meet up with Liz again, but the time wasn't right. He wanted to build up a better father-daughter relationship with Iona, though he was sure he was fighting a losing battle. Much had been spoiled by Mammy and her destruction of his character, and now he faced rearing a teenager who had little respect for him.

And he still laid down the law. Da had told Iona she had to be home by nine o'clock and there was no negotiation. At fifteen, however, Iona didn't like coming home to an empty house when Da was on back shift; it was too eerie for her. When Iona told Sally and her parents her curfew was nine o'clock, they suggested she stay at their house until Da returned from his shift at ten-thirty or thereabouts. But he would have none of it. The weekend was one thing, but it was too late when she had school the next day. Rather than trying to understand, he put forward a cold ultimatum.

'Here's the deal. If you want to stay out later, leave your key on the sideboard before you go out,' he announced.

He was telling her if she wasn't home by nine, not to bother coming home at all. Yet again, it was all about black and white, no grey areas and no opportunity to meet half way. His efforts at getting closer to Iona were rapidly diminishing.

What Da didn't realise was that Sally's parents had already talked about taking Iona under their wing and offering her a room once she was sixteen in a matter of months. When Sally opened the door to a crying Iona the day she had been told to leave her key on the table, there was no more discussion; Iona was invited to stay indefinitely and Sally's parents would deal with Da.

He arrived home to find Iona's key but no note; he guessed where she was.

The following day, he visited Sally's house and spoke to her parents. He could see they were able to give Iona a bed and make sure she was safe. Iona shook her head when he asked if she would come back. Knowing he was beaten, Da offered to pay for her keep until she was sixteen, then left with his tail between his legs.

After a while in the city, I moved back to our hometown and got a local job. Iona left school and, within a few months, found herself a secretarial position in a nearby town. She was independent, sharing a flat and didn't need Da and his strict measures to lead a fulfilled life. She had sporadic contact with him, mainly through me.

With no one else in the house, Da became even more lonely and restless. His visits to Sam and Jen became more frequent. Visits to Bob and Sarah had stopped around the time Mammy went through her second operation and he felt it was inappropriate to pop in to see Liz. He had never fixed her boiler, or the broken tables, and assumed someone else had done the outstanding jobs. During a quick call to Bob before Mammy passed away, he had explained how ill she was and that he'd hoped to pass by, but that never transpired. They had briefly mentioned Liz, but with no genuine conviction. Now and again his mind wandered, wondering how she was and what she was doing with her life.

Da was surprised that thoughts of Liz prompted memories of Mammy. He reflected on their life and, for the first time, considered how difficult it must have been for his late wife. Months after Mammy passed away, Jen had pointed out the pressure of bringing up children on a limited budget and in an era when women were expected to be subservient to their men. He hadn't realised that Mammy might have felt as trapped as he had. Sam suggested that if she had had the psychiatric help now available, she might have dealt with life in a calmer way. Da struggled with his feelings when he had to admit to himself that he hadn't always been an understanding husband; in fact, he had been as unemotional and as strict as his own father. That kind of attitude didn't go down as well in the 1970s as it had in the 1930s. He wondered if he had been locked in the dark ages.

Da told me he had prayed and asked for forgiveness. He made a promise to God that, if he ever got the chance of happiness with a partner again, he would alter his way of thinking. He got up from his knees a changed man.

As he continued to spend time in the city with Sam and Jen, he popped in to see Bob a couple of times. They mused over how quickly the time had flown and caught up with news. Da was interested when he learned Liz was thinking about selling the tea-room and more than delighted to hear she was still single.

He looked out her phone number and remembered his promise to God.

Epilogue

Iona and I became involved in long-term relationships; this brought us closer. I told her that Da had begun to socialise and about Liz. Iona was surprised but happy because she too had known what it was like to be alone and isolated.

Da met with us and, over coffee, said he'd like to introduce us to Liz. When he did, we loved her immediately. She was around for almost a year when Da proposed. By the time they married, she was in her late forties and he was in his mid-fifties. But before the big day, he had asked her a question.

'Would you ever hit me if you were arguing with me?'

She was astounded and told him that she'd never touched another person in anger and it was highly unlikely she would start then. Into the bargain, she never argued with anyone.

He thrived on the kindness and pampering she put his way. They were able to socialise because of her pleasant and inviting nature. She talked him through his disappointment when things went wrong and explained how anti-social it was to dominate the company by bringing out the Bible. She was a Christian; she was an angel according to everyone Da spoke to, including me and Iona.

They married. It was ironic that on the day of their wedding, I had to borrow a car which ended up being a pile of rust and wouldn't start. I was late and missed the church service. I never saw my da walking down the aisle but I made it for the meal and the celebrations. Even stranger, Iona gave birth to her first baby at the same time that Da and Liz were married and never saw any part of their special day. It was as though we were abandoning him, but nothing could have been further from the truth. We were supporting him. It was just that life got in the way.

Peace reigned in our family at last.

Many years later, Liz busied herself preparing a special birthday party for Da. Family and friends gathered to celebrate. Da's brother, Uncle Grant, set up games for the children and adults.

Da and Liz were put in the spotlight when it was their turn to answer quiz questions on how well they knew each other, a Mr and Mrs type game. He was sent out and Liz was put on the hot seat. Uncle Grant asked her some questions about what colour Da's toothbrush was and what his favourite aftershave was. Then the final question came.

'When Adam gets angry, in which of these three ways does he deal with it? Does he a) slam a door, b) go in a huff or c) raise his voice?'

Liz didn't have to think for long; she slowly shook her head. 'But Adam *never* gets angry.'

I looked around. Everyone was smiling. My mouth fell open and I had to stifle a retort.

'OK, let's bring Adam in now and see if he agrees with your answers.'

Correct on toothbrush colour, correct on favourite aftershave and, when asked how he dealt with his anger, he wore one of the nicest smiles I had ever seen. 'But I *never* get angry!'

The dizzy feeling from a lifetime of damage, chaos and violence rushed through my head. I watched the guests clapping and beaming at Da and the woman who had changed his life. I knew it would be a long time before I could tell my story of a paradise lost. The folk who knew him probably wouldn't believe it anyway.

The End

www.ingramcontent.com/pod-product-compliance
Lightning Source LLC
Chambersburg PA
CBHW071154070526
44584CB00019B/2788